The French Revolution

HISTORICAL CONNECTIONS
Series editors
Geoffrey Crossick, University of Essex
John Davis, University of Connecticut
Joanna Innes, Somerville College, University of Oxford
Tom Scott, University of Liverpool

The French Revolution
Rethinking the debate

Gwynne Lewis

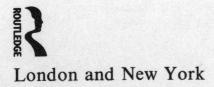

London and New York

First published 1993
by Routledge
11 New Fetter Lane, London EC4P 4EE

Simultaneously published in the USA and Canada
by Routledge
29 West 35th Street, New York, NY 10001

Reprinted 1995

Typeset in 10 on 12 point Times by Witwell
Printed in Great Britain by Clays St Ives plc

British Library Cataloguing in Publication Data
Lewis, Gwynne
  French Revolution: Rethinking the Debate.
  – (Historical Connections Series)
  I. Title II. Series
  944.04

Library of Congress Cataloguing in Publication Data
Lewis, Gwynne
  The French Revolution: rethinking the debate/Gwynne Lewis.
    p.   cm. — (Historical connections)
  Includes bibliographical references and index.
  1. France—History–Revolution, 1789–1799. 2. France–History–
Revolution, 1788–1799–Historiography. I. Title. II. Series.
  DC148.L44   1993
  944.04–dc20   92–44015

ISBN 0–415–05466–4

Contents

Series editors' preface

Historical Connections is a new series of short books on important historical topics and debates, written primarily for those studying and teaching history. The books will offer original and challenging works of synthesis that will make new themes accessible, or old themes accessible in new ways, build bridges between different chronological periods and different historical debates, and encourage comparative discussion in history.

If the study of history is to remain exciting and creative, then the tendency to fragmentation must be resisted. The inflexibility of older assumptions about the relationship between economic, social, cultural and political history has been exposed by recent historical writing, but the impression has sometimes been left that history is little more than a chapter of accidents. This series will insist on the importance of processes of historical change, and it will explore the connections within history: connections between different layers and forms of historical experience, as well as connections that resist the fragmentary consequences of new forms of specialism in historical research.

Historical Connections will put the search for these connections back at the top of the agenda by exploring new ways of uniting the different strands of historical experience, and by affirming the importance of studying change and movement in history.

David Blackbourn
Geoffrey Crossick
John Davis
Joanna Innes

Preface

This book is divided into two parts. Part I provides an interpretation of events covering the causes and course of the Revolution; Part II focuses more specifically upon the controversies surrounding the economic, social and cultural policies associated with the Revolution.

Throughout the text, I have used the terms '*marxisant*' and 'revisionist' to describe the approaches of certain historians. The former includes all those who have accepted the main conclusions of the 'orthodox' (fundamentally marxist) interpretation of the Revolution established by Georges Lefebvre and Albert Soboul, which dominated revolutionary studies until the 1960s. I have used the latter term to describe only those who have explicitly rejected this 'classic historiographical tradition', preferring instead the 'revisionist' theses of historians such as Alfred Cobban and François Furet. My Conclusion will make it abundantly clear that significant differences of interpretation can be found *within* each 'school', and that many historians would not wish to be identified with either. In a purist sense, of course, all historians are 'revisionists', each generation keen to 'revise' the work of its predecessor, but to ignore the existence, since the 1960s, of two competing camps, *marxisant* and revisionist, is to pretend that history can be written in an ideological vacuum, a conceit I have never favoured. Some would argue that to identify *marxisant* historians with the political philosophy of socialism and 'revisionist' historians with liberalism or liberal/conservatism would be going too far. I would, however, be prepared to take a few strides in that direction.

Gwynne Lewis
University of Warwick

Part I

1 Capitalism, colonies and the crisis of the *ancien régime*

Financial crisis

As a result of the Seven Years' War (1756–63), Great Britain asserted her superiority over France as a world power. French influence had been swept out of Canada, effectively undermined in India, and challenged in the West Indies. From 1763 to the battle of Trafalgar in 1805, the bitter pill of defeat stuck in French throats, helping to explain her misguided and financially ruinous foreign policy, including the bizarre decision to send soldiers of the absolute French monarchy to assist republican American colonists in their war of independence against Great Britain. From Choiseul in the 1760s to Vergennes in the 1780s, policy-makers at Versailles usually chose the path of revenge, convinced, as were the British in the eighteenth century, the Germans in the nineteenth, and the Americans and the Russians in the twentieth, that to be a 'great power', one had to be a 'world power'. Choiseul, secretary of state for war throughout most of the 1760s, put it bluntly when he wrote that

> in the present state of Europe it is colonies, trade and in conse-
> quence sea power, which must determine the balance of power upon
> the continent. The House of Austria, Russia, the King of Prussia are
> only powers of the second rank, as are all those which cannot go to
> war unless subsidized by the trading powers.[1]

One may hypothesise that if the Bourbon monarchy had successfully modernised its society and government then it might have sustained the cost of being a world power in the late eighteenth century: after all, the Third French Republic was to create an overseas empire second only to that of Britain a century later. But it did not, and this failure in foreign and domestic policy, allied to the accident of poor harvests, helps to explain the timing of the French Revolution in 1789.

Certainly France appeared to merit her place in the Imperial sun. On the eve of the Revolution, her population of 28 million inhabitants was three times greater than that of her English rival. Conquest on the battlefield (allied to shrewd marriage alliances) had added the outlying provinces of Normandy, Brittany, Burgundy, Languedoc and Provence to the central Capetian core of the kingdom before the arrival of the first of the Bourbon kings, Henry IV (1589–1610); others, Franche-Comté and Lorraine, for example, were to be added during the reigns of Louis XIV (1660–1715) and Louis XV (1715–74). During the course of the seventeenth century, and particularly as a result of the policies of Louis XIII's ministers, Richelieu and Mazarin, power had been increasingly centralised, ultimately at the Court of Versailles, a safe distance from the *frondeur* city of Paris. Reaching its apogee during the reign of Louis XIV, the religious, administrative and judicial rays of the Sun King had blinded most opposition to the Absolute Monarch. From the King's Council, all executive, legislative and judicial power radiated out, through the agencies of the Sovereign Courts, the Intendants, *sub-délégués*, and the royal officers of justice to reach every city, town and village in France. One has to enter a note of caution at this point: the heat of the Sun King was undoubtedly fierce at the centre, but in the peripheral provinces, given the fact that it took over a week for messages from Versailles to arrive in Bordeaux or Marseille, government officials had to compromise with local power. None the less, royal power was a reality, one which could also be felt in the pulpit, from Notre-Dame to the humblest wayside shrine. For the king chose his archbishops and bishops, the pope simply conferring his spiritual blessing upon them. France was a Catholic state, and, although it housed a few hundred thousand Protestants and a few thousand Jews, only Catholics enjoyed full civic rights. Absolutist and Catholic, the Bourbon State was also 'feudal': in theory, all land was owned by *seigneurs* who were, in turn, all vassals of the king.

All this 'in theory'. In practice, as the eighteenth century advanced, the monarchy was undermined by powers ancient and modern. A medieval relic – the Estates-General of the realm – would provide the political platform from which the deputies would stumble into revolution in 1789. Then there were the provincial estates, like those of Brittany and Languedoc, which still defended their 'historic rights and liberties'; or the thirteen medieval *parlements*, effectively silenced under Louis XIV, but which, under his successors, periodically flexed their wasting judicial and administrative muscles. The jurisdiction of the *parlement* of Paris covered one-third of the kingdom, and by refusing to register royal edicts which met with its disapproval, it could seriously undermine the credit – financial and political – of the Crown.

Apart from the king's principal officers like the Intendants, whose influence was most powerful in the central regions of the kingdom (the *pays d'élection*) although they were certainly not without influence in the more recently acquired provinces of Brittany, Languedoc or Franche-Comté (the *pays d'états*), tens of thousands of official judicial and administrative posts had been sold to individuals who were allowed to treat them like family heirlooms, so long as they paid the Crown for the privilege. Venality of office, the historic act of mortgaging the Crown's power for cash mainly to pay for its military aggression during the bloody seventeenth century, was to become an increasingly awkward obstacle to reform.

The same point can legitimately be made about the way taxes, direct and indirect, were collected; 'farmed out' to some of the wealthiest men in France, with the result that a goodly proportion of the king's revenue went into building, or rebuilding, castles on the banks of the Loire. Almost everything in France appears to have been 'farmed out' for ready cash – the king's finances, government posts, seigneurial estates, church tithes, all providing jobs and incomes for an entire army of estate-agents, financial and legal experts. 'Leeches of the poor' they may have been, but they are absolutely essential to an understanding of the way in which the *ancien régime* functioned. Apart from the recruiting sergeant, the most hated 'leech' was the tax-collector, money being the life-blood of most communities. Admittedly, financiers were obliged to run a completely outmoded and socially regressive system: the chief government tax, the *taille*, was arbitrary and inequitable, with most nobles *and* many bourgeois escaping payment altogether; additional taxes like the *capitation* and the *vingtièmes* were targeted at the privileged orders but, more often than not, missed; the clergy escaped taxation altogether, offering the occasional gift, the *don gratuit* instead. The levying of these direct taxes fell to the wealthy *receveurs de taille*; indirect taxes on drink and many other commodities including salt (the *gabelle*) which, due to the wildly differing rates levied from one region to another, represented the most hated tax of all, were 'farmed out' to financial combines, which also negotiated special loans for the government, all of which provided wonderful opportunities for creative accounting. It seems appropriate that employees of the influential Farmers-General should have been called *croupiers*.

These historic restraints which hedged in the theoretical divinity and absolutism of the Bourbon monarchy were not, in themselves, sufficient to explain the political collapse of the 'Old Regime' (as the deputies in 1789 would describe the period before 1789). Many ministers and advisors, conscious of the dangers, were working to shore up the edifice by adjusting to the demands of an increasingly commercial socio-economy. Many tracts were written on the need for a 'revolution' in government. As we shall see in the next chapter, a dress rehearsal for 1789 may be thought to have been staged in 1771. The more far-sighted finance ministers of Louis XVI, from Turgot to Calonne, endeavoured to modernise the taxation system, but, before their projects could be implemented, they usually fell foul of court intrigues or the resistance of the privileged orders, often one and the same thing. On the eve of the Revolution, Necker, the government's chief finance minister – he was never called *comptrôleur-général* because he was a Protestant! – described the taxation system as 'a real monstrosity in the eyes of reason'.

Reason, this was the word which tripped lightly off the tongue of most reformers: it was the word we most often associate with the Enlightenment. This is not to argue that the ideas of the Enlightenment 'caused' the French Revolution. The study of history should not be concerned with laying down single-track lines from one set of points to another, passing chronological stations *en route*. In the first place, most of the standard texts we associate with the Enlightenment had been published before Robespierre was born; in the second, the movement was extremely disparate and multi-faceted, with atheists, freemasons and Catholics all claiming to be 'enlightened'. The argument in Montesquieu's *Esprit des lois* (1748) was relativist and elitist: different forms of government suited different countries; nobles, as represented in the *parlements*, provided a salutary check on royal despotism. Like Montesquieu, Voltaire had drunk deeply at the well of the English Enlightenment, associated, in the main, with the ideas of Locke and Newton. Living the life of a *seigneur* at Ferney near the Swiss border by the 1760s, this mocking sage had absolutely no love for the masses. He was a dramatist, an historian, above all a tireless opponent of injustice and intolerance. His work for the rehabilitation of Jean Calas, the Protestant brutally broken on the wheel in 1762 for the alleged murder of his son, represents a landmark in the history of religious toleration in Europe. Two years later, Beccaria would write his influential treatise, *Of Crimes and Punishments*, demanding a more humane system of justice. Voltaire and Beccaria were fully paid-up members of the 'Party of Humanity'.

Far more radical than Montesquieu and Voltaire in their approach were the editors of the *Encyclopédie*, Denis Diderot and Jean d'Alembert: the former's brilliant analyses of French culture and society contained more than one whiff of 'modernity'. Launched in

1751, the *Encyclopédie* had grown to seventeen volumes by the mid-1760s, providing the greatest and most practical minds of the age with a platform for their knowledge and opinions; for the mid-eighteenth-century *philosophe* was 'inclined as much to practical reform as to utopian musings'.[2] If the classic works of Montesquieu and Voltaire had drawn their inspiration from the past, the articles published in the *Encyclopédie*, accompanied by state-of-the-art engravings and illustrations, pointed the way forward to a more rational, scientific and humane period in European history, one which our century has done little to advance. But perhaps the Panglossian fascination with progress through the twin forces of science and reason which most followers of the Enlightenment exhibited, the determination to explain human endeavour and behaviour through 'laws' adapted from the natural sciences, took too little account of the forces of irrationalism which Voltaire himself sought to confront as he left, at the end of *Candide*, 'to cultivate his garden'. For most *philosophes*, however, it seemed but a short and positive step to tread from Newton's world of physical certainties to Condorcet's confident hope of human progress through a rational education system. Science and reason were the keys which would turn the locks and liberate France from her feudal past. Benjamin Franklin was more famous in France for his lightning-conductor than for his experiments with democracy in America, whilst that 'hero of two worlds', the marquis de Lafayette, would become a firm believer in Mesmer's theories on 'animal magnetism'. Some *philosophes*, like Condillac, professed opinions which related consciousness to the workings of a machine, leading many thinkers in the direction of atheism. God may still have been in his heaven, but he was certainly being transformed into the 'Great Watchmaker in the Sky'. Freemasons, whose numbers grew apace during the second half of the eighteenth century, preferred the term 'Architect of the Universe'. All this rationalism and science seemed totally incompatible with the metaphysics of monarchy, the magic and the mystery, the pomp and circumstance of Versailles, as indeed it was.

We have decided to provide Jean-Jacques Rousseau with a short paragraph of his own not only because his ideas were, for the most part, increasingly at variance with those of his fellow-geniuses (Jean-Jacques was convinced that he, at least, was one), but because his influence permeated so many fields of intellectual and artistic inquiry. An auto-didact and sometime music-copyist, Jean-Jacques was the kind of awkward personality you would decide not to invite to dinner, only to regret it later. He was the novelist who altered people's attitude to reading (*La Nouvelle Héloise* (1761) evoked an emotional storm);

the educational psychologist whose pioneering work *Emile* (1762) can still be found on the reading-list of most departments of education; the political theorist who still provokes the admiration and/or contempt of critics on the left and right of the political spectrum. His *Contrat Social* (1762), an exercise in political theory, emphasised the overriding importance of direct democracy through popular assemblies, placing ultimate sovereignty in the hands of the people, but, it should be noted, with the 'Legislator' interpreting their wishes at the centre, a troubling concept. Central to his thesis was the proposition that man – like the great majority of *philosophes*, Jean-Jacques thought that a woman's place was in the home weeping over novels like his *La Nouvelle Héloise* – was born good; it was urban, over-refined society, not the curse of Adam, which had tainted him. He was further of the opinion that the 'General Will' (to be distinguished from the will of the majority, though few then or since fully understood how) embodied the general good.

Is it a coincidence that the high peak of the Enlightenment in the 1750s and 1760s coincided with a period of very considerable economic growth in France? Marxist historians such as Albert Soboul certainly posited an *indirect* relationship between the widely perceived growth of capitalism and the intellectual 'take-off' of the Enlightenment: 'the philosophers explained that man must try to understand nature so that he could more effectively control it and could increase the general wealth of the community'.[3] For *marxisant* scholars, socio-economic change provides the soil in which the seeds of the Enlightenment could germinate. There can be no doubt that the advance of science and technology did encourage new thinking, new *applied* thinking on the relationship between science and society. Most historians would also agree that there was a relationship between population growth – around 7 million more citizens in 1789 than in 1700 – economic success and social crises. And population growth was, in all probability, associated with climatic changes – the need to understand the natural sciences again – involving far less severe winters and fewer catastrophic crop failures, particularly during the middle decades of the century. More mouths to feed, more food to feed them with, more hands to produce manufactured goods; capitalism, in its commercial and nascent industrial forms, was provoking change, occasionally violent protest, in all but the more secluded rural recesses of eighteenth-century French society. It was certainly provoking discord and debate amongst the king's ministers and civil servants in the corridors of Versailles.

Bearing in mind the crucial point that agriculture provided three-quarters of the gross national product – in other words, there were a great many rural recesses in France – economic research, or rather computerisation of old research, indicates that during the eighteenth century French manufacturing and industrial performance was comparable to that of Britain, at least until the late 1770s when the 'take-off' was sustained in the former country, but 'aborted' in the latter. Around this time, textiles accounted for over half of the value of all industrial production. The production of woollen goods increased by almost 150 per cent between the beginning and the end of the eighteenth century; the number of looms producing high-quality articles in the silk capital of the world, Lyon, doubled during the same period. Nîmes, 250 kilometres due south, was producing over one hundred different articles for the cheaper end of the market – silk stockings, handkerchiefs, ribbons to grace the feet, hands and heads of ladies and gentlemen from Paris to Peru. Even in the 'leading sector' of the industrial revolution, cotton, French production increased sharply after the 1740s, recording growth rates of almost 4 per cent per annum. In and around Rouen, 'the Manchester of France', production of cotton goods tripled between 1730 and 1750. To the north-east, towns like Lille were also becoming transformed by the impact of the textile revolution. To the south, reaching its highest levels of output around the middle decades of the century, the woollen industry of Languedoc, centred on towns such as Carcassonne, Clermont-de-Lodève and Sommières, provided work for tens of thousands of peasant-artisans. Even in the heavy industrial sector, France was producing more cast iron than England by the 1780s, and, at around three-quarters of a million *tonnes*, its annual production of coal was starting to look, well, almost respectable, although it was still under a tenth of British coal production.

However, the jewel in France's economic crown was not Lyon, or Rouen, or even Paris, but Saint-Domingue (today known as Haiti), emphasising the remarkable growth of France's overseas trade and the supremacy of commercial over industrial capitalism. The volume of her foreign trade more than doubled in the course of the eighteenth century; trade with her colonies increased tenfold! With its thousands of imported slaves producing cheaper sugar and coffee than the English West Indian islands, Saint-Domingue alone had monopolised three-quarters of France's lucrative colonial trade by the time of the Revolution. The English traveller, Arthur Young, was deeply impressed with the visible and recently acquired wealth of Atlantic ports such as Nantes and Bordeaux: 'we must not name Liverpool in competition with Bordeaux', although, liberal as he was, he fails to relate the joys of merchant wealth to the miseries of the black slaves upon which they were largely based.[4] Henry Swinburne, visiting Marseille in 1776, provides us with the best description of these bustling eighteenth-century ports:

> The commerce of Marseille is divided into a multiplicity of branches, a variety of commodities are fabricated here, or brought from the other ports and inland provinces of France to be exported, and numerous articles of traffic are landed here to be dispersed in this and other kingdoms.[5]

The lustre of France's overseas and colonial trade has led some historians to suggest that there were two distinct types of economies in France: one, thriving until the Revolution, anchored on the great ports and rivers of France, the other, increasingly sluggish after the mid-1770s, based in the France of the small provincial town and its huge, rural hinterland.

This neat division has some merit, not the least of which is its simplicity. The situation was more complicated, however, as the recent emphasis on the development of an eighteenth-century, 'consumerist' society indicates, one which affected most French people, although certainly more immediately in Paris, the major manufacturing towns, like Lyon, Lille and Rouen, and the prosperous ports of the Atlantic and Mediterranean coasts. Symbolic of the advance of this kind of economy was the fact that workers had already taken to the habit of popping into their local bar for a *café au lait* on their way to work, whilst their wives may have been putting on their bonnets to visit the place de Grève, site of public executions on most weekdays, but transformed on Mondays into a second-hand clothes market where women with a few *sous* to spare might haggle for hand-me-downs from the rich merchant's or lawyer's wardrobe. Daniel Roche notes that, during the eighteenth century, the commercial life of Paris was focused increasingly upon the needs of the *classes populaires*, a society which

> had its habits, rhythms, manners, and pitches like the pillars of les Halles, Saint-Esprit, the quai de la Ferraille, quai de l'Ecole, under the Pont-Neuf; they tramped the town, cutting, restitching, taking apart and remaking the ordinary garb of the people.[6]

That acute observer of the social mores of the Parisians on the eve of the Revolution, Louis-Sébastien Mercier, bemoaned the fact that consumerism was beginning to cover up class distinctions, with 'the wife of the petit bourgeois seeking to imitate the wife of the marquis and the duke'.[7] Recent work upon the growth of a 'consumerist society' in France, one which pre-dates the Revolution, reinforces the importance of capitalism, again in its commercial guise, as eroding the bases of the old order.

However, there is overwhelming evidence to suggest that the French economy on the eve of the Revolution was failing to satisfy demand, at the right price, both domestic and foreign. During the late 1770s, France's balance of trade would move into deficit; the huge textile industries of Brittany, Normandy and Languedoc would suffer a serious decline, which, in certain sectors, would prove terminal. In Languedoc, the 'golden age' of the woollen industry had already passed away by the 1760s, whilst the silk trade was severely disadvantaged by the Spanish embargo on French imports after 1778. The growth of capitalism was an international, not a French, phenomenon. As Professor Sidney Pollard has shown, European industrialisation developed on a regional, not a national basis, challenging the old economic structures.[8] The serious downturn which characterised the fortunes of the flourishing wine industry in France during the 1780s – another example of a change in consumption patterns – aggravated the situation: between 1778 and 1788, profits from wine were halved; in the champagne region around Rheims, tax-collectors were speaking of a crisis 'the like of which had not been known for thirty years'.[9] Undoubtedly, a series of poor harvests reduced internal demand in a country which depended so heavily upon agriculture for its gross national product. But there were other reasons, possibly of greater importance. For example, foreign competition, from Prussia, Switzerland, Italy, as well as from Spain and, of course, England, adversely affected the crucial textile sector. When in 1786, the Eden Treaty with England opened up French markets to certain English exports, howls of outrage could be heard from cotton wholesalers and merchant-manufacturers from Rouen to Lille. There were, of course, notable exceptions to the rule of recession: the colonial trade, for example, continued to serve the greater glory of rich merchants in the Atlantic ports.

The lack of a cutting, competitive edge to defend its economy from foreign competition can be explained, in large measure, by the workings of an economic system better-suited to medieval than to modern forms of industry, or, as François Crouzet expressed it a generation ago, France did not experience a *technological* revolution comparable to that which was taking place in Britain. With its substantial population providing a steady supply of cheap labour,

France's *per capita* production was falling behind, particularly as the century drew to its close.[10] Recent historians have coined the term 'proto-industrial' to describe this small-scale system of production which unlike the 'cottage industry' of the medieval type, supplied markets throughout Europe *and* the Americas, and which was undoubtedly one of the channels through which capitalist and cash values penetrated the countryside, and, very importantly, provided the type of cheap goods which the new consumerism required. It was, in many ways, a sophisticated system with its domestic workers supplied with raw materials by merchants or middlemen, backed up in turn by bankers and wholesale dealers with trading houses in ports throughout the known world.

For all its sophistication, however, as well as its more human and, possibly, humane aspects, there is little reason to doubt that proto-industrial forms of production were becoming increasingly cumbersome and less cost-effective by the late eighteenth century. In Great Britain, mechanisation was beginning to transform production methods: in 1789, she had over 20,000 spinning jennies, 9,000 mule jennies and 200 'factories' of the Arkwright model; France had only 1,000 spinning jennies, no mule jennies and fewer than 10 mills *à la Arkwright*.[11] In the Alès region of south-eastern France, an entrepreneur named Pierre-François Tubeuf, struggled for almost two decades to modernise the coal-mines of the region only to be defeated on the eve of the Revolution by the resistance of small landowners and proto-industrial workers who sought, and received, support from the powerful *seigneur* of the region, the marquis de Castries, minister of the navy in the 1780s and confidant of Marie-Antoinette.[12] Just two examples among many of the contrasting manufacturing and industrial systems of France and her neighbour. We should add to this the fact that whilst millions of acres of land were being enclosed in Britain between 1760 and 1820, across the Channel millions of small farmers were ploughing (much to the chagrin of Arthur Young!) a very different furrow for the future of French capitalism.

This is not to argue that the French economy 'failed' because it did not slavishly imitate the action of the English. There is more truth to the proposition that it failed because its government, inextricably bound up with the social *mores* if not the political reality of a post-feudal society, felt obliged to deal with things as they were, not as critics like Arthur Young, who saw everything through English eyes, thought that they should have been. French theorists, like the *physiocrats*, were convinced that wealth was founded upon land, not, like Adam Smith, upon the production and exchange of goods. And there was good reason for this. Four out of five persons in France in 1789 were living in hamlets or villages of under 2,000 inhabitants. The peasantry owned – or, at least, *they* thought they 'owned' – two-thirds of all the land cultivated in France. Most wealth in France was invested in land, and would continue to be based upon land well into the nineteenth century: to ignore this crucial point is to misunderstand the French Revolution. Land was a safe form of investment, but the vast number of smallholdings allied to antiquated methods of production meant that agricultural productivity was significantly lower than in Britain. The big difference between British and French agriculture, however, was the twin burden of government and feudal taxes which weighed most heavily upon the peasant. Arthur Young was vehement in his denunciation of feudal survivals: most economic historians agree, with varying degrees of emphasis, that the potential wealth and productivity of France was being held back by the palsied, but still powerful, grip of feudalism.

For the land to be cleared of its tangled, feudal past, the political and judicial structures which reflected that same past would have to be changed. France still operated within the antiquated juridical framework of a post-feudal society. The Estates-General, when it met in 1789, would still be divided into the medieval trinity of those who prayed, those who fought, and those who worked – the First Estate representing the clergy, the Second the nobility, with the rest of society lumped together as the 'Third Estate'. The task of clearing what contemporaries referred to as the 'débris of the past' was not going to be easy, given the control exercised over society and government by the privileged orders. At the end of the eighteenth century, the nobility, comprising around 25,000 families – in other words, not much more than 1 per cent of the total population of France – still owned over a fifth of its land. Certainly the nobility was riven with internal division, explicable by differences of wealth, office and education. A social world separated the powerful and pensioned noble at Versailles (there might have been 1,000 court nobles) from the proverbial, impoverished Breton *seigneur* on his 'nimble nag', whilst a similar distance divided the latter from the 'nobility of the robe', this service nobility which had bought its way through the purchase of official positions in the judiciary and the civil service into the ranks of the privileged. Tim Blanning suggests that 6,500 individuals acquired titles of nobility during the course of the eighteenth century which meant that 'about a quarter of the total French nobility was of very recent origin'.[13] Even as a 'caste', let alone a 'class', the French nobility was fractured and exceedingly fractious, but then few thought in terms of social class until writers like the *abbé* Sieyès boldly bridged the conceptual gulf, long before Karl Marx, between social and economic realities and political power. Before 1789, the aristocracy controlled, if they did not monopolise, political power, with nobles of various lineages and wealth filling most of the key positions in the French army, navy and judiciary.

The nobility were no less evident in the upper reaches of the Catholic Church; indeed, the wide social gulf between 'aristocratic' archbishops, bishops and abbots, and the lower clergy drawn from the non-aristocratic, occasionally popular ranks of society would be crucial to the outbreak of the Revolution, when the majority of the lower clergy in the First Estate would join the Third Estate to create the 'National Assembly' in the summer of 1789. According to Ralph Gibson, the Catholic clergy as a whole numbered around 170,000 – including 60,000 parish clergy, 26,500 monks, and 55,000 nuns.[14] Although religious observance varied enormously from one region to another – strong in parts of the west, north-east and south, weak in most large cities, and many regions immediately south of Paris – the Catholic Church governed the daily lives of the vast majority of French men and women. Protestants counted for only 2–3 per cent of the total population; Jews an even lower percentage, although the influence of both communities, particularly in trade and finance, was higher than their numbers would suggest. Neither Protestants nor Jews enjoyed equal civic rights with Catholics before the Revolution. In addition to its control of education and social welfare, the Church owned between 6–10 per cent of the land in France and collected the first tax to be levied on the land, the *dîme* or tithe. France was truly a Catholic country, in the village as well as at Versailles. The failure of the revolutionary elite to appreciate the power of the Church is crucial in any explanation of the 'failure' of the Revolution to achieve its stated objectives.

The growing ranks of the bourgeoisie – their numbers may have trebled between 1660 and 1789 – may be divided into their landed, commercial and industrial, and professional sectors. They owned a quarter of the land of France; their influence and their values increasingly permeated the countryside through the purchase of *seigneuries*, through the action of the cultured naturalist or linguist who sought to classify, in accordance with the example of the *philosophes*, the human and natural species which inhabited the countryside, that 'other world' of eighteenth-century France. In terms of hard cash, 'most industrial and almost all commercial capital, amounting to almost a fifth of all French private wealth, was bourgeois owned'. A great deal of capital had been invested in the purchase of venal offices, whose value increased, not declined, during the course of the eighteenth century. William Doyle, a sharp critic of *marxisant* theories of history, concludes that 'their share of national wealth was enormous' and that the 'ultimate source of this enrichment was the extraordinary commercial and industrial expansion of the eighteenth century'.[15] In cultural terms also, as we shall see in our final chapter, bourgeois tastes and attitudes were challenging the former cultural hegemony of the aristocracy. No wonder the *abbé* Sieyès, in his famous pamphlet *What is the Third Estate?* could write:

> In vain the people of privilege close their eyes to the revolution that time and the force of things has brought about; it is real none the less. Formerly the Third was serf, the noble order everything. To-day the Third is everything, the nobility but a word; but under this word has crept illegally, through the influence of false opinion alone, a new and intolerable aristocracy; and the people has every reason not to want aristocrats.[16]

But who were Sieyès' 'people'? In theory, everyone who was not a noble or a cleric; in practice the educated and property-owning middle classes. This gap between theory and practice would become unbridgeable during the Revolution as the mainly urban bourgeoisie, whatever the weak state of their class consciousness before 1789, acquired the philosophical certainty and the political power that they, not the nobility, not the less affluent craftsman or peasant, and certainly not the propertyless and labouring poor, were now the natural leaders of society – *la nation, c'est nous*, as they might have put it. Revisionist historians have been very keen to push the idea that, instead of a developing *bourgeois* consciousness, representatives of the nobility and the wealthy bourgeoisie were 'fusing' to form a new social elite, the *notables* of the nineteenth century. Guy Chaussinand-Nogaret provides the most articulate and challenging version of this theory which argues, indeed, that the nobility, not the bourgeoisie, were in the vanguard of change:

> Profoundly altered in its substance, rejuvenated in its blood, stimulated by the intrusion of capitalism, released from isolation by the absorption of the integrating notion of merit, the nobility had become the chosen instrument of a revolution in social elites.[17]

Colin Lucas provided a less radical, and rather more convincing, version of this 'elite' thesis in his article 'Nobles, bourgeois, and the origins of the French Revolution', which placed more emphasis on the influence of the bourgeoisie and the exclusion of too many of their qualified members from the corridors of power.[18] There can be no question that, through a shared involvement in the socio-economic and cultural changes which were transforming the structures of French society, nobles and bourgeois were 'fusing'; it is equally clear that what separated nobles from bourgeois was far more important than what united them, and nowhere was this more evident than in the anti-quated political and juridical division of society into 'estates'.

At the lower end of the wide spectrum of the bourgeois class, tens of thousands of master-artisans in the scores of corporations into which the Parisian and provincial world of craft work was divided would also have considered themselves to be 'bourgeois', particularly if they were urban-dwellers. Their employees, whether journeymen (*compagnons*), 'the largest group of people employed in the eighteenth-century French trades with no corporate status', or apprentices, would have been excluded.[19] But again, Michael Sonenscher's research emphasises the fluidity of this world of work, the networks of kinship and patronage, particularly of the journeymen as they travelled from town to town, or from master to master, learning their respective trade, enmeshed in the moral and juridical, as well as the economic, world of eighteenth-century France. Pressures for higher levels of production during the eighteenth century adversely affected the working practices of skilled workers, whether textile-workers, hat-makers, furniture-makers or printers. Before 1789, their protest would be couched in the language of the eighteenth-century artisan, a language of 'freedom' appealing to moral and political concepts of justice, although the reality of their more straitened circumstances was directly linked to the operations of capitalism and international trade. The degrees of hardship experienced would obviously depend on their trade, the region they inhabited, and the cycles of boom and recession, but many would carry their grievances into the Revolution, in which political crucible they would be moulded into 'sansculottes'.

The regulations of the 1760s, allowing semi-skilled or unskilled workers in the countryside to operate free of guild restrictions (though not of government regulations concerning the quality and size of work produced), aggravated the problems confronting the traditional urban craft worker whilst further dissolving the boundaries between town and countryside. The fact that France had a vast reservoir of labour in the countryside upon which to draw, as well as its traditional attachment to the land, helps to explain the different patterns of industrialisation pursued by Britain and France. In France, the labour force was scattered over a wide geographical area, living and working in small towns (almost 300 with populations of over 5,000 inhabitants) and villages (four out of five people living in communes of 2,000 or under). Apart fom large conurbations like Paris (pop. 700,000) and Lyon (150,000), it was a dispersed society of small farms and workshops, the ideal environment for the development of the village sansculotte.

However, by far the most numerous social category in France on the eve of the Revolution was the peasantry, which accounted for roughly 67 per cent of the population. Individual peasant properties were most numerous in poorer regions; in the richer cereal-growing regions, such as the Beauce south-west of Paris, estates were in the hands of noble and bourgeois owners. Nothing is easier than to slot 'peasants' into certain categories – the very select group of rich *laboureurs* or *gros fermiers* (tenant-farmers) at the top, merging in individual cases into the category of a 'rural bourgeoisie'; the *petits propriétaires*, or *haricotiers* as they were known in parts of the north, in the middle; the *métayers* (sharecroppers), very widespread in parts of the west, the centre and the south; and the increasingly numerous *journaliers* or *travailleurs de terre* (day-labourers) at the bottom. However, once one begins to examine in detail a particular region like that around Rouen in Normandy or Nîmes in Lower Languedoc we find many 'peasants' engaged on a wide range of activities, from spinning and weaving, to silk-rearing and coal-mining. In addition, tens of thousands of landless peasants from certain regions, such as the Auvergne or the Limousin, or parts of Brittany, migrated every autumn to find work in Paris, in provincial towns or in the richer cereal or wine-growing regions. Indiscriminate use of the term 'peasant' disguises more than it reveals. Our idea of the rustic inhabitant with a scythe in his hand and manure on his boots must be adjusted to encompass the fact that hundreds of thousands of 'peasants' in eighteenth-century France owned looms or spinning-wheels and worked, particularly in the winter months, for merchant manufacturers, or middlemen, who provided them with the raw materials. As Peter Jones remarks: 'Most artisans lived in the countryside, and most rural artisans were part-time peasants.'[20]

It might be argued that historians, *marxisant* or revisionist – the former fascinated in the 1950s and 1960s with artisans, the latter more recently with 'elites' –: have focused too much on the members of the three estates which met in 1789. There was a 'Fourth Estate', one which encompassed possibly half of the entire population, and one which was destined to play a formative role in shaping the course of the Revolution, if only because of the fear they inspired in the breasts of the possessing classes. It was an estate of poverty, those who lived by 'an economy of makeshifts'. They were consumers rather than producers, the first to starve, the first to lose their jobs in times of hardship. They included the hundreds of thousands of farm labourers, unskilled textile workers, second-hand dealers, water-carriers, odd-job men, the 30,000 or so prostitutes who lived in Paris and who were buried unceremoniously, at night, in the paupers' graves of the Clamart cemetery. The statistical basis of the crisis experienced by the urban and rural poor during the reign of Louis XVI was provided by Ernest Labrousse over half a century earlier, a crisis which saw the price of basic commodities rise by 45 per cent between the 1730s and the 1780s (with an even sharper rise during the late 1780s) whilst wages only rose by just over 20 per cent. The textile crisis of the 1770s and 1780s was one which affected, in varying degrees, urban and rural workers, driving many on to the roads as beggars. These were the 'dangerous classes' who terrified sensitive observers of the French social scene such as Louis-Sébastien Mercier. Commenting on the widening gap between the very rich and the very poor in Paris, Mercier wrote in his *Tableau de Paris*: 'the people seem to be a separate body from the other estates of the realm', adding that 'one can find more money in one house in the faubourg Saint-Honoré than in all the houses of the faubourg Saint-Marcel'.[21] The immense, and widening, gap between *les gros* and *les petits* was to play a key role in pre-revolutionary and revolutionary politics.

2   The birth of the Republic, 1787–92

It took the Americans over seven years to create their republic: it would take the French over seventy years before a republican system of government was able to sustain itself for more than a few bloodstained years. The fundamental reason, from a political standpoint, for the protracted birth of the first French Republic, finally announced in September 1792, was the resistance of the monarchy and its sympathisers abroad, as well as in the outlying French provinces of the west and the south-east, not just to the idea of a republic, but to the moderate solution of a constitutional monarchy. Louis XVI and his Austrian wife, Marie Antoinette, encompassed their own downfall by elevating their political ideology (as 'totalitarian' as anything dreamed up by Rousseau), their caste and monarchical calling above that of 'their' people. This is to oversimplify, as subsequent modifications to this important point will suggest, but this would be the reluctant conclusion drawn by the new breed of national politicians by the summer of 1792, the great majority of whom were monarchists at heart, republicans only by default.

Recent historians have insisted that modern forms of politics, the concept of 'public opinion', even of 'the nation', had emerged long before 1789, during the 1750s and 1760s in fact. John Bosher suggests that during this period, 'the public was unwittingly preparing to govern France by election and debate, by assembly and committee, by pamphlet and journal, by legislation and organization'.[1] The twenty-eight volumes of the *Encylopédie, ou Dictionnaire raisonné*, published in these decades, reflected the discovery of a new world order, founded upon science and reason. 'Progress' was the new buzz-word, validated by the discovery that life-forms, including man in society, were *evolving*. Darwin and Marx would be children of this Enlightenment mode of thought. In the political arena, appeals to history were made to validate arguments on all sides, the main discovery being that 'the

LIVERPOOL
JOHN MOORES UNIVERSITY
AVRIL ROBARTS LRC
TEL. 0151 231 4022

people' were also on the march. In the *Lettres historiques sur les fonctions essentielles du Parlement* which the monarchist Louis Le Paige had published in 1753–4, reference could already be found to the concept of a French 'nation'. The birth of the first French Republic was preceded by a fairly lengthy, and complicated, pregnancy.

The more far-sighted ministers of the Crown were very aware that something was stirring in the body politic, something which called for radical change. From 1771 to 1774, Maupeou, Louis XV's chancellor, had spearheaded a royal coup against the *parlements*, effectively abolishing their powers of resisting royal legislation. This was 'Enlightened Despotism' in practice. But resistance to Maupeou's brand of 'ministerial despotism' had been widespread, inside and outside the Court, the entire episode tending to increase the popularity of the *parlements* as 'guardians of the people's liberties', despite the fact that they represented little more than their own privileged selves. The fundamental question was, could the French Crown negotiate the change from a society dominated by the aristocracy to one in which the bourgeoisie would, at least, share power? The auguries were never good. Upon his accession to the throne in 1774, Louis XVI, anxious to court popularity, had recalled the *parlements*, thus undoing almost all of Maupeou's work. Critics were now convinced, on the one hand, of the 'despotic' designs of the Crown – a touch of administrative 'despotism' at this point in time would have been salutary – but, on the other, of its inability to see things through to the bitter end. As Keith Baker concludes: 'Many of the arguments given currency in the aftermath of the Maupeou coup circulated in the pamphlet war of 1787 and 1788; the debate over "despotism" that opened in 1771 found its eventual resolution seventeen years later in 1789.'[2]

If Maupeou's coup, or rather its failure, had ultimately weakened rather than strengthened the power of the monarchy, Vergennes' foreign policy had brought the political and economic crisis in France to a head. Choosing to fight a colonial *and* a continental war, tied to Austria by the 'Diplomatic Revolution' of 1756, France had experienced the decline of her influence in North America and India, had witnessed Prussia, Russia and her new ally Austria set about the dismemberment of Poland, whilst her old allies, Sweden and Turkey, were losing out to Russia in the Baltic and the Crimea. Tim Blanning suggests that 'This collapse on the Continent might just have been thought worthwhile if it had been counterbalanced by a colonial revival of compensating proportions.'[3] Vergennes thought that the American War of Independence from Britain (1775–83) provided the opportunity France was seeking: 'Providence had marked out this moment for the humiliation of England', he told a sceptical king.[4] It was all an illusion. England's political system may have been corrupt, but its social, economic and parliamentary system – as well as its geography – was far better geared to face the challenge of the new world of European imperialism and modern capitalism.

Meanwhile, here was France, an absolutist monarchy, helping to create a republic in America! Her domestic and her foreign policies were running on completely different tracks. The creation of the American Republic may have been an immediate defeat for Britain; it proved to be a long-term disaster for France. When Tom Paine, one of those eighteenth-century 'citizens of the world' and father of modern British radicalism, who had played a very significant role in the American war, arrived in Paris in 1789 he would be welcomed 'as an American hero, his portrait being seen even in country inns'.[5] From a financial standpoint, involvement in the American war had led France to the brink of bankruptcy. When, in the autumn of 1787, after several years of confrontation between the princely House of Orange and republican 'patriots', Prussia, supported by Britain, invaded Holland on behalf of the former, the French were impotent to intervene. Holland, in 1787, was the geographic intersection where an anachronistic foreign policy collided with a ruinous financial programme. Altogether, the American involvement cost the French State over a billion *livres*, although Necker, the popular finance minister, had successfully masked this awful truth in the first balance sheet produced during the *ancien régime*, the *Compte rendu* of 1781.

Having continued his predecessor's policy of borrowing until no more money was forthcoming, the new *comptrôleur-général*, Calonne, decided late in 1786 to implement, through a hand-picked 'Assembly of Notables', the most radical programme of reform ever produced by the Court. The Assembly met for the first time on 22 February 1787: 144 representatives of 'the Great and the Good', divided into seven committees, each chaired by a prince of the blood. However, instead of rubber-stamping his proposals, it actually provoked the *political* crisis that led to the downfall of the monarchy. As a result of a combination of political infighting, factional intrigue and privilege, Calonne's two main proposals – a tax to fall on all landowners, *irrespective of rank*, and the creation of new provincial assemblies – were effectively rejected. Both sides appealed to the public for support, Calonne in April with his *Avertissement*, which stated that whilst taxes would undoubtedly increase, the privileged orders would carry the heaviest burden. But ministers who did not command the support of monarchs could do nothing under an *ancien régime* system of government, particularly one under the pusillanimous Louis XVI: on 8 April, Calonne was shown the door. His successor, Loménie de Brienne, also failed to secure any meaningful reform on the essential issues and, on 25 May, the Assembly was dismissed. Averting immediate collapse through the time-honoured expedient of loans at high rates of interest, de Brienne felt that he had little option but to return, cap in hand, to the *parlements*.

However, having sunk at least their front teeth into the monarchy, the privileged orders, strongly entrenched in the *parlements*, were not going to relax their grip now. Between the summer of 1787 and the autumn of the following year, the Court, the thirteen *parlements*, led by the Paris *parlement*, and the majority of the provincial estates, led by those of Brittany, fought a running battle which, despite one last throw of the monarchist dice by Chancellor Lamoignon underlined the indecisiveness of Louis XVI and his divided Court. On 6 August 1787, the Court endeavoured to force the Paris *parlement* to register the new edicts concerning the land tax and provincial assemblies. The following day, the *parlement* declared such a move 'illegal' and, in traditional manner, was exiled to Troyes. At the beginning of September it was back, and more or less on its own terms – agreement to a temporary tax but no permanent land tax or provincial assemblies controlled by the Third Estate. The following spring, the old political charade was repeated. On 3 May 1788, the Paris *parlement* issued its famous document entitled 'The Fundamental Laws of the Kingdom'. Since it declared that only an Estates-General of the realm could sanction the levying of new taxes, explaining to a stunned monarch that France had always been a constitutional monarchy in disguise, the Court decided on one last show of strength, an 'action-replay' of Maupeou's *coup* in 1771. On 8 May, Lamoignon, issued the famous 'May Edicts'. These, by creating a new body for the registration of royal legislation (a *Cour plénière*), and by increasing the judicial powers of the *grand bailliage* courts, effectively nullified the judicial and legislative authority of the *parlements*.

In 1771, Maupeou had sustained his *coup* for three years; Lamoignon's reforms lasted just three months. Again, money was for Louis XVI to be the root of all evil: on 8 August, the Court had to rescind the 'May Edicts', and agree to the convocation, for the first time in 175 years, of an Estates-General, scheduled to meet in May 1789; ten days later, the government officially announced that it was bankrupt. At the end of August, the popular financial expert, Jacques Necker, was recalled. By this time, however, the crisis had assumed national dimensions. During that fatal summer of 1788, towns and villages throughout France, spearheaded by the *parlements* and *ad hoc* assemblies of citizens, were drawn into the debate, provoking riots in the town of Rennes in Brittany, the 'Day of the Tiles' in Grenoble, Dauphiné, when, on 7 June, troops were attacked by protesters from rooftops. On 21 July, the extremely influential Vizille Assembly, held near Grenoble, produced a prototype of the Estates-General of 1789, with the Third Estate having the same number of representatives as the First and Second Estates combined, with voting carried out by head rather than by order. This was no longer a political game reserved for the privileged few.

Mention has already been made of the increasing importance of 'public opinion'. During the crisis of 1787–8, the public was given a more articulate voice, that of the Press. In 1777, France's first daily newspaper, the *Journal de Paris*, had appeared. However, according to Jeremy Popkin,

At least 767 pamphlets were issued between 8 May and 25 September 1788, with an additional 752 between 25 September and 31 December of that year, but this was only a prelude to the 2,639 titles that appeared during the election of the deputies to the Estates-General in the first four months of 1789.[6]

No wonder that during the summer of 1788 the political crisis which had broken out with the closure of the first Assembly of Notables in May of the previous year began to assume revolutionary proportions. 'Public opinion' was on the march. During the next twelve months, hundreds of thousands of starving and unemployed French men and women would be recruited to its colours as economic recession and harvest failure transformed a political crisis into a political and social revolution.

A crucial stage in this transformation was the announcement by the Paris *parlement*, on 21 September 1788, that the regulations concerning the composition and proceedings of the proposed Estates-General should be the same as those which had governed its last meeting in 1614. At a stroke, the pretence that the *parlements* represented the wider interests of the nation vanished. Other privileged bodies widened the gap between political reality and the defence of privilege. In November, a hastily reconvened meeting of the Assembly of Notables supported the *parlement*, whilst, the following month, the princes of the blood issued a memorandum aimed at stiffening Louis XVI's backbone by reminding him of his duties to his faithful aristocracy in general and to the sanctity of feudal dues in particular. Revisionist historians suggest that, because a number of liberal nobles and clerics supported, in the influential Committee of Thirty for example, the developing programme of the Third Estate, one should not take this kind of resistance too seriously. Albert Soboul, on the other hand, argued that the essential *political* struggle leading to the outbreak of Revolution in 1789 was the clash between a nation in embryo and a Bourbon State which had failed to adapt itself to modern conditions: 'All attempts to reform this administrative structure had failed because of the resistance of the aristocracy, a resistance which had been channelled through the institutions which the nobles firmly controlled, the *parlements*, the provincial estates, the clerical assemblies.'[7] This analysis carries considerable weight.

The most revolutionary act of the Bourbon monarchy was performed on its deathbed. Having previously conceded the principle of doubling the representation of the Third Estate (though not the crucial point of voting by head), the regulations governing the elections to the Estates-General, published on 24 January, proved to be extremely democratic. François Furet believes that these regulations were central to the emergence of a 'national' assembly the following summer.[8] The elections did produce a majority of parish priests in the First Estate, whilst around one-third of the noble Second Estate turned out to be 'liberals' of various hues. The successful candidates to the Third Estate were lawyers, landowners and office-holders, leavened with a sprinkling of renegade nobles like Mirabeau, a combination of intellectual radicalism and social conservatism. Just as revolutionary, in the circumstances of the summer of 1789, was the decision to follow the traditional precedent of asking every citizen in France, directly or indirectly, to present the king with a list of grievances. The participation of Frenchmen, from humble peasant and artisan to great noble, in the preparation of these *cahiers de doléances* was to provide the deputies to the future National Assembly with a blueprint for the renovation of the country, highlighting as they did, albeit in occasionally contradictory manner, the necessary shift from a decayed feudal society to one more congenial to the development of liberal capitalism.

The Estates-General began its deliberations at Versailles on 5 May. Primed ideologically by the demands contained in the *cahiers de doléances* as well as by the issues raised during the press and pamphlet war of the previous year, conflict with the Crown was inevitable. It came the very next day when the Third Estate refused to meet as a separate order. In that most influential of pamphlets, *What is the*

Third Estate?, the abbé Sieyès had warned of the fight to come, reminding the Third Estate,

> that it is today the national reality, of which it was formerly a shadow; that during this long transformation, the nobility has ceased to be the monstrous feudal reality that could oppress with impunity; that it is now no more than a shadow and that this shadow will seek in vain to terrify a whole nation, unless this nation wants to be regarded as the vilest in the world.[9]

A 'National Assembly' or nothing became the order of the day, an objective secured by the lack of a coherent policy on the part of the Court (the death of the dauphin on 4 June did not help matters), and the defection to the Third Estate of sympathisers from the clerical, then the noble estates. On 17 June, the Third Estate officially transformed itself into 'the National Assembly'; three days later, as a result of the famous tennis-court oath, the Assembly swore that it would not dissolve until it had provided France with a new constitution. Ten days later, the Court caved in and ordered all deputies to join the infant 'National Assembly'. The political revolution of 1789 had been accomplished, though not totally secured.

That security, against a counter-*coup* by the Court, was provided by 'the people' – artisans and craftsmen in Paris, peasants and artisans in the countryside, often led by radical bourgeois figures. At the beginning of July, Louis (or was it Marie Antoinette?) decided to play his trump card – armed force. Troops were moved into Paris from the provinces. The king was right to assume that he could no longer rely upon the local Parisian militia, the *Gardes Françaises*, despite, or perhaps because of, the fact that they had killed dozens of rioters at the end of April when the property of a wallpaper manufacturer named Réveillon had been ransacked. Réveillon had made some injudicious remarks about wages during an electoral meeting, underlining the explosive combination of political upheaval and economic distress. On 12 July, news reached Paris from Versailles that Necker had been dismissed. For the majority of Parisians, Necker was the man who could secure food in a crisis at affordable prices and we must recall that the price of bread on 14 July was the highest recorded in the eighteenth century. For the deputies, now huddled at Versailles with no means of defence, Necker was a man who honestly sought (as indeed he did) a peaceful transition to a constitutional monarchy along British lines. That most famous event in European history, the storming of the Bastille on 14 July, resolved the impasse between the Court and the National Assembly, but it did so at a price.

Henceforward, the Parisian crowd would haunt the battlements of the bourgeois Revolution, reminding deputies that, in revolutions, the bullet is as important as the ballot.

The *quatorze juillet* supplied the *coup de grâce* to absolute monarchy in France. Its significance, however, goes far deeper than this. It provoked, or rather it strengthened, a whole series of mini-revolutions throughout France, as a result of which effective power, administrative and police, passed, in a very messy way, from the supporters of the *ancien régime* to the 'patriots of '89'. In Caen, power was placed in the hands of a General Committee after the town's inhabitants had stormed its own 'Bastille', the eleventh-century castle overlooking the town which had been built by William the Conqueror.[10] However, the corridors of revolutionary power, at central and local level, were frequented, in the main, by the propertied and educated classes, amongst whom one could find a good sprinkling of liberal nobles and clerics. In many towns an armed force was created, such as, for example, in Montpellier in the south-east: its 'Légion de Montpellier', had been formed as early as 18 April, more out of fear of the starving poor than of the reactionary Court.[11] Central to an understanding of the history of the French Revolution from 1789 to the advent of war in the spring of 1792 is the fact that those deputies and civil servants entrusted with the awesome responsibility of carrying out a revolution, the scale of which few of them had foreseen, were as frightened, at crucial times more frightened, of the millions of poor, hungry and unemployed Frenchmen and women as they were of the king. Indeed, if the defence of property and 'law and order' were to be the central issues, as they rapidly became, they needed Louis XVI far more than they needed the propertyless masses.

This fear, endemic amongst the propertied classes and born of long experience, was exacerbated by the greatest peasant rebellion to sweep through France in the eighteenth century – the 'Great Fear' of 1789. Widespread opposition to the levying of feudal dues had begun as early as 1788; the discussions over the *cahiers de doléances* had increased the general discontent, which continued sporadically in some regions like the south-west well into 1790. We shall analyse the social and economic reasons for this broader anti-seigneurial 'peasant war' in chapter four. The peak of the 'Great Fear', however, occurred during the three weeks immediately following the fall of the Bastille, emphasising again the *politicisation* of the longer-term socio-economic problems confronting rural society. According to Peter Jones, it was the 'socio-economic and political conjuncture of 1789 which made possible the amalgamation of at least five regional distinct fears into one over-arching "great fear" which travelled the length of the kingdom'.[12] It was, in large measure, this massive rural rebellion which prompted the deputies in Paris, during extraordinary and emotional scenes of self-abnegation, to pass one of the most important pieces of legislation to emerge during the Revolution – the decrees of 4–11 August which wrote *finis* to the decayed bastions of feudalism and privilege in France, as well as firing the first whiffs of grape-shot over the bows of other *ancien régime* monarchies in Europe. If 14 July had dealt a death-blow to the political authority of Bourbon France, the night of 4 August destroyed its social and administrative base.

However, from the beginning of the Revolution, serious contradictions began to emerge between the rhetoric of liberty, equality and fraternity and the reality of a revolution led by a wealthy, propertied elite. It was one thing for noble and clerical deputies on 4 August, intoxicated by the revolutionary moment, to declare that the feudal regime was 'abolished in its entirety', quite another for the landowning deputies, in the sober light of day, to agree to the end of all seigneurial payments. Abolition of the church tithe and *personal* dues smacking of the feudal past, yes, but seigneurial dues relating to land contracts, definitely not. PROPERTY is the key-word which unlocks the major mysteries of the Revolution. Although the Declaration of the Rights of Man, passed on 26 August 1789, begins with the famous formulation that 'All men are born free and equal in rights', we have to recall that article seventeen declared property to be 'inviolable and sacred'. Edmund Burke, in his famous work, *Reflections on the French Revolution*, spotted the main contradiction which was to be the curse of the Revolution – the incompatibility of general, universal, or what Burke called 'metaphysical' truths with the very particular, individual property rights of the ruling elite.

The Constituent and Legislative Assemblies – the former sitting between August 1789 and September 1791, the latter from September 1791 to the overthrow of the monarchy on 10 August 1792 – were cautious about pursuing too radical a programme. Indeed, although it is something of an exaggeration, one could say that the main problem confronting the deputies was how to *end* the Revolution rather than how to propel it towards more radical goals. The main objective, after all, was not the destruction of the monarchy in favour of popular democracy, but the transformation of the outmoded institutions associated with absolute monarchy into a 'republican' form of government propped up by property-owning shareholders with the king as Managing Director. However, the Parisian crowd, *les petits*, were always standing at the elbows of the deputies anxious to remind them, *les gros*, of their revolutionary duties. On 5–6 October 1789, women, prompted by the old combination of politics and hunger, marched to Versailles and brought the king, the queen and the dauphin back to the capital. Henceforth, the monarchy was to be a prisoner of Paris, and let us repeat that it was women, not men, who had effected this extraordinary *coup*. A few days later, the Constituent Assembly passed a law aimed at outlawing, on pain of death, 'unofficial' demonstrations, a revealing illustration of the triangular struggle for power between the Court, the Crowd and the Constituent Assembly, which characterised the first two years of the Revolution. This struggle was to become more acute, and more bloody, as the deputies endeavoured to translate 'metaphysical' propositions into hard legislation. Why? The answer to this crucial question – one which goes to the heart of the failure of the Revolution to produce a peaceful and parliamentary solution to the revolutionary crisis – revolves around three issues: the emergence of a counter-revolutionary movement, at home and abroad: the profound divisions produced by the religious policies of the Assembly, linked, as they were, to the massive debts inherited from the *ancien régime*; and the related rise of a 'popular movement' in Paris and the provinces.

If a lasting compromise between the Court and the National Assembly was to be effected, the aristocracy, including the higher clergy, would have to be placated. Complications on this front arose from day one, for immediately following the 14 July, the comte d'Artois, together with other close relatives of the king, had chosen to emigrate; many more were to follow, including important, but moderate, monarchist supporters like Malouet and Mounier, after the March to Versailles in October. The emergence of a counter-revolutionary movement was to complicate beyond measure the task of peaceful change, particularly since Marie Antoinette, whose brother was the Emperor of Austria, was far more sympathetic to the counter-revolution abroad than to the revolution at home. From his *émigré* court in Turin, the comte d'Artois organised a counter-revolutionary movement as early as the autumn of 1789; the king's brother, the comte de Provence, would also set up a camp for *émigrés* in Coblentz. Both d'Artois and Provence, supported by an increasing band of faithful nobles and their camp followers, exerted enormous pressure on Louis XVI not to concede too many powers to the bourgeois lawyers beavering away at the mammoth task of reshaping France in the thirty-odd committees set up by the Constituent Assembly. However, the root-and-branch reorganisation of the country necessarily involved the root-and-branch eradication of its decayed feudal structures.

Worries on the part of the deputies concerning the 'popularisation' of the Revolution, may be seen in the proposals for the new constitutional monarchy which left the king with considerable powers. He could choose his own ministers outside of the Assembly; he was given the right of holding up legislation for several years by the provisions of the 'Suspensive Veto', agreed to as early as 11 September 1789. Some advocates of a strong executive, such as the venal Mirabeau, fought unsuccessfully to increase these powers by giving the king the right to declare war and peace, but they had lost the argument by the end of September when the original constitutional committee was reorganised. For, by this time, nothing could hide the crucial fact that the king would henceforth have to rule on behalf of, and through the medium of, the French people, not on behalf of the aristocracy. In case there should be any doubt on this matter the Assembly, on 10 October, decreed that henceforward the king would be 'Louis, by the grace of God, and the constitutional law of the State, King of the French'. Louis XIV might be heard turning in his tomb. For nothing could really mask the essential fact that power, including the power of the purse, had effectively passed from the Court to the *representatives* of the French people, the crucial point being that it would be the Assembly which initiated legislation, its decisions only being passed on to the king for his royal sanction. Furthermore, there was to be no upper house, no House of Lords on the British pattern through which the king might exercise his influence and patronage. This unicameral system underlines the anti-aristocratic ethos in which the new France was being constructed. It was this radical attack upon aristocratic privilege which would make any peaceful transfer of political power to an aristocratic/bourgeois elite, along the lines of the British 'Glorious Revolution' of 1688, virtually impossible.

For, whether at the centre or on the periphery, the old legislative and administrative organs of an aristocratic system of government were being dismantled. The process involved the end of noble privilege and with it 'the whole structure of provincial, local, and municipal government'.[13] In November 1790, all ranks of nobility would be abolished. Gone were the *parlements*, the provincial estates, the diocesan assemblies through which much local government had been conducted. Gone too was the centralisation of power, which had been articulated by the Intendants since the days of Louis XIV. The Revolution, in its first phase, would decentralise most administrative and political power. The law of 14 December 1789 creating the new municipalities took power away from the king's representatives, as well as, in many instances, from the local *seigneur* and *curé*, and, through the principle of elections, handed it over to local taxpayers. This change was one of the most important to occur during the first momentous year of the Revolution. It was supplemented by the law of 22 December 1789 which divided the country into departments, eventually fixed at eighty-three, each with its subdivisions of districts and cantons, an administrative structure which has lasted, in essence, to the present day. However, in the turbulent and bewildering period of the first two years of the Revolution, this handing over of power to the people was to be fraught with dangers; counter-revolution could, and did, find a home in many a locality. The contagion would be particularly virulent during electoral periods as the French breathed the new and somewhat heady elixir of political participation. The first significant manifestation of counter-revolution in France occurred in Nîmes in south-eastern France on 13 June 1790 during the first elections for seats on the departmental and district councils. Several hundred people would be butchered in this bloody encounter.

It is instructive, however, that the violence in Nimes occurred outside the bishop's palace. If the decentralisation of France gave the counter-revolution the political space it needed if it were to develop into a serious threat, it was to be the Civil Constitution of the Clergy, passed in the Assembly on 12 July 1790, which actively promoted that development. A new constitution for the Church was inevitable after the deputies, in order to resolve the central issue of the State's colossal debts, had decreed the seizure of all ecclesiastical property on 2 November 1789. The debate over this act – the most revolutionary and divisive measure to be introduced save for the decree 'abolishing' feudalism on 4 August 1789 – was long and heated; after all, property was property, whether it belonged to a peasant or a priest. It was decided, however, somewhat speciously, that Church lands had only been held 'in trust', and since the fledgling nation had no trust any longer in the Church – deemed to be yet another bastion of aristocratic privilege, at least at the top – an exception to the iron law of property-rights, now 'inviolable' if no longer 'sacred', could be admitted. It was a disastrous decision, on at least three counts: the related introduction of the *assignat* – paper money backed by the value of Church lands used to pay off the State's creditors – would lead to massive inflation, thus aggravating the socio-economic crisis which had afflicted France since the 1780s; the decision not to call a General Council of the Church made it easier for the pope to denounce the new religious settlement, which he was to do in April 1791; and the provision in the new Constitution for the clergy to be *elected*, by atheists and Protestants as well as by good Catholics, to their posts came as manna from heaven to counter-revolutionary leaders throughout France. If the counter-revolution abroad would rest upon the pretensions of princes, the counter-revolution at home would rest, primarily, upon the prayers of the faithful. When, on 27 November 1790, the deputies passed a law forcing clerics to swear an oath to uphold the Constitution, almost all the higher clergy and around half of the lower clergy refused.

The threat of major disaffection from the Revolution, already being transformed in a few areas of the west and south-east of France into the beginnings of a Catholic and royalist counter-revolution, provided ammunition for those popular leaders in Paris and the provinces who, through the medium of the Press and the Popular Society, were becoming increasingly worried about the conservative furrow being ploughed by the wealthy and educated elite in the Constituent Assembly. Their fears had been considerably increased by the decision of the deputies concerning voting rights. It had been decided as early as 22 December 1789, that, although all men were equal (women, of course, were still outside the political pale), men who owned property (active citizens) were more equal than those who did not (passive citizens). It was eventually decided that to qualify as a voter one had to pay the equivalent in direct taxes of three days' work; this group of around 4 million, would then choose electors (around 50,000 in number) who qualified by paying the equivalent of ten days' work. To qualify as a deputy, one had to be very rich indeed, paying over 50 *livres per annum* in taxation. This, according to the radical and sanguinary journalist Jean-Paul Marat, was the 'aristocracy of wealth' which was in danger of replacing the old 'aristocracy of birth'. This view was shared by the fringe of deputies who sat on the left of the Assembly, amongst whom a certain Maximilien Isadore de Robespierre was beginning to make quite a name for himself. From the Jacobin Club, situated in the rue Saint-Honoré, a stream of advice and guidance flowed out to the hundreds of clubs which were appearing in almost every town, large and small, in France. From the spring of 1790, activists in the capital could also attend the meetings of the Cordelier Club, which, partly because of its low entrance fee, attracted a far more popular audience than its Jacobin rival. As they made their way to its meetings, members might well have been seen reading a copy of Jacques Hébert's scurrilous and scandalous newspaper the *Père Duchesne*.

The summer of 1791 proved to be the first real turning point of the Revolution, marking the beginning of the end of the conservative attempt to graft the frail shoots of liberal capitalism on to the decaying trunk of feudalism. The most ominous event was the Flight to Varennes, that instructive and abortive attempt by the royal family on 21 June 1791 to join the counter-revolution abroad. Who could now place any faith in the fiction of a 'constitutional monarchy'? The answer was the vast majority of deputies in the Constituent Assembly who concocted the fiction that the king had been 'abducted', such was their need of royal legitimation for the Constitution of 1791 which they had laboured long and hard to produce. But the fiction had worn thin. Although he would hang on until the final overthrow of the monarchy in August 1792, a deputy such as Pierre-Victor Malouet, who strove to effect a liaison between the Revolution and the Court, had clearly seen the writing on the wall. His *Club Monarchique*, harried by the Jacobins and their sympathisers, had been forced to disband a few months earlier,[14] whilst the Jacobin Club would divide into its radical and conservative wings, the latter, led by Barnave, Lameth and Du Port, assuming the name of the *Feuillants*. Just a day after this important split was made public on 16 July, the Cordelier Club organised a rally in the Champ de Mars to drum up support for the creation of a Republic. The dreaded word had been spoken. The reponse of the authorities, led by Lafayette as Commander of the National Guard, was to fire on the crowd of demonstrators. Long before the Terror, the Revolution had begun to devour its own.

Events abroad confirm the significance of that long, hot summer of 1791. The outbreak in Saint-Domingue of the black revolt led by one of the legendary figures of black history, Toussaint-Louverture, marked the beginning of a bloody war which was to alter the island's history for ever.[15] But of more immediate relevance was the growing strength of the counter-revolution abroad and its links with foreign powers. Samuel Scott has noted that, following the abortive Flight to Varennes, what was still the Royal Army began to disintegrate: between 15 September and 1 December 1791, no fewer than 2,160 French officers would emigrate.[16] Confronted with growing resistance, external and internal, it was a singular act of folly on the part of the Constituent Assembly, which ended its herculean labours on 20 September 1791, not to allow its members to stand for election to the Legislative Assembly, charged with the task of implementing the decisions of its predecessor. The early leaders of the Revolution were long on theory, but very short on political experience. However, although it would be quite wrong to dismiss the Legislative Assembly as an ineffective and unproductive body, its work was, from its earliest sessions, to be overshadowed by the threat of war. From 1787 to 1792, the leaders of the Revolution had wrestled unsuccessfully with the contradictions inherent in the attempt to impose a conservative, but liberal solution upon a recalcitrant aristocracy and a responsive, but increasingly disenchanted public. From 1792 to the advent of Napoleon Bonaparte seven years later, war would not altogether change the agenda of the Revolution; it would, however, produce more radical and revolutionary responses.

3   War, revolution and the rise of the nation-state, 1792–9

From 20 April 1792 to the battle of Waterloo on 18 June 1815, an entire generation of French men and women was to know nothing but war, or the threat of war. This single, salient fact was to condition the political, economic, social and cultural life of France throughout the 1790s and 1800s. In this chapter we shall examine the major political and ideological issues of the period, emphasising the inter-relationship between the survival of the Revolution, confronted by powerful internal and external enemies, and the increasing authority of the 'nationalised' and centralised French state.

Our emphasis upon war brings us immediately to the heart of the matter concerning recent interpretations of the significance of the Revolution, and, in particular, of the Jacobin Terror of 1793–4. Was the failure of parliamentary democracy in France by 1799 a direct consequence of total war: in other words, was the liberal, constitutional Revolution doomed after April 1792? Or was the political and ideological inheritance shared by the early leaders of the Revolution so 'totalitarian' in character, so impregnated with Rousseauesque notions of 'the General Will' that any attempt, irrespective of war, to create a pluralist, liberal parliamentary system was doomed from the start? For Tim Blanning, the former argument is more persuasive: 'war inflicted permanent social, economic and political damage . . . ending with the destruction of the Revolution'.[1] For one of the leading revisionist historians, François Furet, the revolutionary elite had drunk too deeply of 'a debased version of Rousseau's philosophy, according to which the sovereignty of the people could be expressed only through a single, indivisible body in full command of all public authority'.[2] Obviously both views are plausible and attractive. One cannot separate the ideology of the Revolution from the fact of war: the infamous guillotine claimed its first victim in the very month that war was declared. Neither can one deny the influence of Enlightenment thought upon important revolutionary personalities, although here the evidence is more specious and open to different interpretations. Both Condorcet and Morellet became opponents of the Revolution.

If one is seeking an explanation for the *political* failure of the 'bourgeois revolution' then Professor Furet's thesis, in particular, devalues both the strength and persistence of the counter-revolution on the right, which itself helps to explain the outbreak of war in 1792, and the popular movement, in Paris and the provinces, on the left, which helped to prosecute a successful war effort. Louis XVI, his relatives, his wife, in particular, as well as leading members of his Court, *were* fighting a political and social battle against the fundamental principles of 1789. If any one group refused to be incorporated in any Rousseauesque, 'universal' system of government, it was the Court, in the Tuileries and abroad, and this political fact offers a more convincing single explanation for the failure of the conservative solution of 1789-91 than any other. It should also be noted that the problems posed by the rise of both the 'right' and the 'left' contributed, in no small measure, to the significant growth of a strong, centralised French State during the 1790s. For all the eddies of revolution and war, one, admittedly winding, current flowing throughout the 1790s may be discerned – the increasing determination of the wealthy, commercial, industrial but predominantly landed elites to 'save' the Revolution, Rousseauesque or not, from the 'radical' popular masses in Paris and as well as from the 'reactionary' popular masses in the counter-revolutionary centres of the Vendée and the south-east. By 1792, *les gros* had become distinctly uneasy about the political and social claims of *les petits*. It was in the pursuit of their objective of reshaping France in their own image that the propertied classes would realise that a strong State was essential. However, widespread political apathy and administrative instability during the late 1790s undermined moves in this direction, creating the political circumstances for a series of *coups d'état*. By 1799, the army had become the only agency which could save both the bourgeois revolution of property-owners, their ranks swollen by the purchasers of church and *émigré* lands, as well as the historic and geographic country of France.

The strains imposed by the first few months of war between France and her enemies in 1792 snapped the increasingly rusty link which had chained the Court, no longer identified with the nation, to the revolutionary settlement. On 27 May, the Legislative Assembly passed a decree involving the deportation of non-juring priests; on 8 June, it called for a levy of 20,000 volunteers from the provinces – the famous *fédérés* – to help defend Paris from its enemies, at home and abroad. Both were vetoed by the king, thus sharpening the nature of the struggle over the feasibility and necessity of a constitutional monarch. Suspicions of the Court were increased when Louis decided to dismiss the first Girondin ministry (March–June 1792), headed by Roland, Servan, and Clavière. The king had been warned, in no uncertain language, by Roland that the Court's decision to veto the Assembly's emergency decrees would undoubtedly provoke social revolution in the country. The tragi-comic prologue to this 'social revolution' was enacted on 20 June when a crowd of sansculottes from the suburbs of Paris rampaged through the Tuileries palace, forcing the terrified king to don a red cap of liberty as a gesture to the menacing crowd. These events forced home the unpalatable truth that if property and status were to be protected, early idealistic notions of 'popular democracy' would have to be jettisoned. The programme of *Feuillant* leaders such as Antoine Barnave or, indeed, that of the prototype Napoleon, the marquis de Lafayette, had been directed against popular involvement in the Revolution in favour of a constitutional monarchy based upon a wealthy, property-owning elite – in short, the English paradigm. Too much attention has been paid to French borrowings from the bank of political theory which the British had founded during and after the Civil War: it was the way that the British elites had retained social and political power in their own hands that attracted wealthy groups like the *Feuillants*. However, the conjunction of political and military events swept away the *Feuillant* option. It would resurface in 1814, but only as an English *diktat* after the holocaust of the revolutionary and Napoleonic wars.

The early months of fighting in 1792 had produced few serious encounters between French and allied troops. However, when 'the invasion came, in August, the almost complete collapse of France, even of fortified towns that should have held out for months, was a shattering surprise'.[3] The potent mixture of betrayal and fear was strengthened by the Duke of Brunswick's Manifesto, which reached Paris on 1 August, threatening the Parisians with dire consequences should the royal family be harmed. It is ironic that it was the monarchy, whose duplicity had helped to provoke this great crisis of the Revolution, which was to become its first victim. In the bloodiest *journée* of the Revolution, in which around 800 royalist defenders and 400 attackers were killed, the Parisian Sections, buttressed by the *fédérés* from Marseille and Brest as well as by the more revolutionary battalions of the National Guard, stormed the Tuileries palace on 10 August, thus provoking the downfall of the centuries-old French monarchy. On 20 September, the Legislative Assembly was replaced by a 'National Convention' elected by universal manhood suffrage. Two days later, the First French Republic was born. The Convention would even introduce a new revolutionary calendar to mark this auspicious event, the first day of the first year of the Republic dating from its birth on 22 September 1792. *Les petits* were marching into the Sections of Paris and on to the stage of history.

The next eighteen months were to reshape the destiny of France, indeed, the destiny of much of Europe, underlining the fact that the French Revolution should not be studied in isolation. A strong State would emerge, albeit a temporary one, founded upon a reformulated alliance between the radical bourgeoisie and the Popular Movement, an alliance which had produced the unity required to overthrow the absolute monarchy in 1789. However, the fall of the constitutional monarchy in August 1792 energised those twin dynamos of revolutionary change, the counter-revolution and the Popular Movement. The princes and *émigrés* abroad, whose numbers had been considerably swollen after 10 August, may not have exerted too great an influence on the foreign powers who, often grudgingly, sheltered them, but there can be no doubt about their malignant influence upon public opinion in France. When, therefore, conspiracies involving an alleged insurrection to be led by the marquis de la Rouerie in the provinces of Normandy and Brittany had been unveiled in July 1792, or when periodic spasms of counter-revolutionary violence erupted in the southern province of Lower Languedoc, the opportunity for moderate and sensible policies to develop was correspondingly diminished. The counter-revolution, internal and external, helped to push France towards war in 1792; its increasingly organised presence polarised public opinion and aggravated the religious strife unleashed by the Civil Constitution of the Clergy in 1790, thus providing political space for radical politicians in the Jacobin Club convinced that France and its Revolution could not be saved without an appeal to popular forces.

There was also space, created by the enthusiasm of revolutionary change inside and outside France, for this still unchained beast, 'public opinion', to roam. From Moscow to Merthyr Tydfil, café-loads of radicals donned the *bonnet rouge* and drank a toast to the infant Republic. In the London Tavern in November 1792, 500 'friends of liberty' sang the Marseillaise and proposed no fewer than forty toasts to the new France, that 'model for all nations'.[4] English, Americans, Dutch, Poles, and Germans flocked to Paris and the rue Saint-Honoré, the international headquarters of the Jacobins. The latter did not initiate an international revolutionary movement in the 1790s; they were part of one. European popular democracy came of age in the 1790s; its manual would be Thomas Paine's *The Rights of Man*. Appropriate, therefore, that Paine should have been elected to the French National Convention. For various reasons, 'republicanism', which had been *à la mode* since the foundation of the American Republic a decade earlier, became the flavour of the month in progressive political circles, not just in France, but throughout much of the known world. Part of the strength of the Jacobin version of popular participatory democracy lay in the fact that it was universal not just French.

In Paris itself, a popular revolution from below had given the Jacobins their launching-pad for success. The majority of the forty-eight sections of the capital, as well as the guard-rooms of the National Guard, had been infiltrated by those 'passive' citizens who had been excluded from the vote in 1791. It was these Sections, through their Central Committee and the Commune of Paris, which had planned the successful revolution of 10 August. When, at the end of the month, news reached Paris of the fall of the fortress town of Longwy, it was again the Commune and its agents, prompted by sanguinary outbursts in the press from Jean-Paul Marat, which had organised the most brutal and horrible event of the Revolution, the September Massacres. Between 2 and 6 September, over 1,200 inmates of several Paris prisons, mostly common criminals but including also 200 priests, were butchered in bloody courtyards. The September Massacres mark a watershed in the troubled history of the relationship between 'the people' and the political elite in France. Popular violence, provoked by foreign invasion and counter-revolution, would have to be tamed, either by constructing an alternative 'official' terror, or by puncturing, once and for all, this myth of a universal, revolutionary will. The Jacobin Terror of 1793–4 was a product, not so much of Enlightenment theorising as of war, and the related twin political forces unleashed by the Revolution itself, popular radicalism and elite – and popular – counter-revolution.

In many ways, the Girondins (occasionally referred to as 'Brissotins' after their leading figure, Jacques Brissot) tried to bridge the gap between elitist and popular solutions to the revolutionary and military crisis. Between September 1792 and June 1793, they struggled to prosecute the internal and external war on behalf of the newborn nation, but became increasingly uneasy about the degree of popular involvement which alone could guarantee a successful outcome, given that, by 1793, France was fighting most of the Great Powers of Europe. During the *journées* of 31 May/2 June 1793, the Girondin experiment ended when the Parisian Sections stormed the Convention to secure the arrest of twenty-nine Girondin deputies, thus paving the way for the installation of the Jacobin Terror, the embodiment of the strong State. Originally, there had been little to distinguish a 'Girondin' from a 'Jacobin': both regarded themselves as supporters of a property-owning democracy and the principle of equality before the law; both were late converts to the belief that a republican form of government was appropriate to France; both sides had sat in the Jacobin Club speechifying like the lawyers and journalists the majority of them were. What then had provoked the bitter and fatal controversy between Jacobins and Girondins after September 1792?

In the first place, the facts of political life rather than ideological disputes. The elections to the National Convention – held at the same time as the September Massacres it must be remembered – had produced a Jacobin clean sweep in Paris, pushing the Girondins into the ill-fitting mould of the 'provincial' or 'federalist' party. Some Girondins, as their description suggests, hailed from the Gironde region of south-west France, representing provincial towns which had been alienated by events in Paris during the summer of 1792, particularly by exaggerated reports of the September Massacres. In Lyon, second city of France and, significantly, political base of the Girondin minister Roland, moderate councillors lost power in municipal elections held in October to the radical faction led by Marie Chalier: 'Amongst the propertied classes the election results were regarded as a further manifestation of the criminal conspiracy which had begun with the September massacres.'[5] The French Revolution was not just about Paris; 'Girondism' was, to a considerable extent, a product of a provincial reaction to events in the capital, a necessarily confused and contradictory one which itself helps to explain the downfall of the Girondists by the early summer of 1793.

Gradually the Girondins, by force of circumstances as much as ideological commitment, became the apologists for a moderate, representative form of democracy, one better tuned to the wishes of the professional, commercial and property-owning elites of France, most of whom still hankered after the security of a monarchy, albeit a constitutional and loyal monarchy. At the end of the day the Girondins gave the impression that they would act tough with the popular masses. Had it not been for the scale of the crisis which was to afflict the Revolution by the spring of 1793, this substitute for the failed constitutional monarchy of 1789–92 might have worked. But there was also a failure of political will. It was the Girondins, not the Jacobins, who were prepared to sacrifice, in a period of acute crisis, the need for a strong State to theoretical speculation about 'democracy' and 'representation'. Girondin vacillation over the fate of the king, imprisoned since 10 August, illustrates this point. Every deputy agreed that Louis XVI was guilty of treason: the only issue to be decided was the price that he should pay for his treachery. The Girondins supported the idea of popular referendum: the Convention voted 424–283 against such a move, and, on 17 January, 387–334 in favour of the death penalty. On 21 January 1793, Louis XVI went bravely to his death in what is now the place de la Concorde. The Girondins had bungled the king's trial, and popular suspicion of them as 'closet royalists' was confirmed. As Robespierre, predicting the creation of the Revolutionary Government some months later, pointed out, 'You are confusing the situation of a people in revolution with that of a people with a settled government.'[6] It was a confusion which lay at the heart of the failure of the Girondins, of the failure of the Revolution to achieve a stable political settlement.

The military crisis of August–September 1792 had launched the second Girondin ministry; that of the spring of 1793 engineered their downfall. On this occasion, however, the situation was exacerbated by the oubreak in March of the greatest manifestation of counter-revolutionary insurrection in the history of the Revolution. Once again, internal and external threats combined to push the Revolution towards more radical extremes. The Vendéean insurrection takes its name from the region of the Vendée in western France, although, at its height, it covered many departments north and south of the river Loire. The link between counter-revolution and war is obvious since the overt and immediate cause of the insurrection was the decree of 24 February calling up 300,000 men between the ages of 18 and 25. In Paris and the provinces, this *levée-en-masse* energised the forces of popular radicalism and popular counter-revolution. In the capital, the Parisian Commune voted on 1 May to raise 12,000 volunteers; the same number of recruits had been promised by the department of the Hérault in the south-east.[7] However, in some parts of France, particularly in the west, the *levée-en-masse* prompted many young men to join the swelling ranks of the counter-revolutionary guerilla bands, which, by the summer of 1793, had been elevated to the status of an *armée catholique royale*. Confronted with weak or uneven resistance, this holy army had swept through towns like Cholet, Thouars and Fontenay and reached the gates of the major western town of Nantes. Meanwhile, the war against the allied powers, which had begun in September 1792 with the famous victory over the Prussians at Valmy, had turned to disaster as first Britain (in February 1793) then Spain (a month later) joined the allied armies to strangle the infant French Republic. For Britain, it was the opening of the Scheldt estuary in the Netherlands to foreign trade and the hope of plunder in troubled French colonies like Saint-Domingue in the Caribbean, rather than the execution of Louis XVI, which had prompted her entry in February 1793. For France, it was to be a momentous decision, a major round in the fight for world, rather than continental, power status which was to end, by 1815, in Great Britain's favour.

With the revolutionary paper money, the *assignats*, falling in value daily, riots for bread and basic food supplies increasing in number and ferocity, with a major civil war inside France and the foreigner once more at her gates, time had run out for the Girondins. On 29 May, the usually cautious Maximilien Robespierre issued a scarcely veiled appeal for insurrection in the Jacobin Club, that hatchery for political *coups*. On 31 May–2 June 1793 the machinery of insurrection was put into gear once again, the Convention invaded and twenty-nine Girondin deputies arrested. A few escaped to the provinces to help organise a 'federalist' revolt which, lacking widespread public support, had petered out by July, or had merged, as in Lyon, with royalist movements aimed at the restoration of the monarchy. The abortive Federalist Revolt of the summer of 1793, which particularly affected hard-hit commercial and textile centres such as Marseille, Nîmes, Bordeaux and Caen, although a damp squib from a military standpoint, is, however, very significant as 'a continued reaction against popular politics, particularly the agent democracy championed by the Parisian sansculottes'.[8] Halted by the regular army at Evreux in the west and Pont-Saint-Esprit in the south-east, the revolt spluttered to an ignominious collapse in July, and with it the Girondin experiment of a 'popular revolution' carried out without the participation of the popular masses. Surviving Girondins would learn their lesson. After 1795, the lower orders would be expelled from the political arena.

From the summer of 1793 to the summer of 1794, the period known to history as 'The Terror', the Revolution was saved from its internal and external enemies, at considerable cost to human life and the infant political democracy of the early 1790s, symbolised by the famous

Constitution of 1793. Published on 24 June, it was not only founded upon universal male suffrage but included the right to public assistance and to education, as well as the 'right to insurrection'. It was, of course, never implemented, since, formalised by the decree of 10 October 1793, the government of France was declared to be 'revolutionary until peace'. The fact that the Constitution of 1793 was stillborn underlines the immense gap – central to an understanding of the Revolution – which separated the political idealism of 1789 from the harsh socio-economic and military facts of life in that summer of 1793 when Jacobins and sansculottes began to dominate the political scene in most towns and villages of France, a sword in one hand, a social policy in the other. The great political paradox of the Year II would be that whilst the Jacobins, desperate to unleash the energies of the nation for war, sought to satisfy the social and economic aspirations of the urban and rural masses, they were also creating the structures of a powerful State bureaucracy, civil and military, which would eventually be used to eject the mass of the public from a participatory democracy.

Not that the Terror of 1793–4 should be identified too hurriedly with the Jacobins: the institutions of the Terror had been created long before Robespierre joined the government on 26 July 1793. Following the downfall of the monarchy, France had been governed by a Council of Ministers supported by committees of the Convention, not the ideal structure for a wartime crisis. It was this crisis which gave birth to the Terror. It was not the Jacobin, but the Girondin-dominated Convention which had created the *représentants-en-mission* to the provinces as well as the Revolutionary Tribunal on 9 March 1793; the same body which set up, on 21 March, those basic units of terror, the *comités de surveillance*, and, on 7 April, the Committee of Public Safety. Furthermore, if one enquires into the origins of the revolutionary relationship between the central government and local municipalities and districts, one must look not to the Jacobins, but to the deputies of the Legislative Assembly, who, given the king's refusal to energise the entire nation for war, had instructed local government to set itself upon a war footing as early as the spring of 1792.[9] The apparent contradiction between the Jacobin theory of liberal democracy – individual rights and the defence of property included – and the facts of the Terror cannot be resolved without reference to the facts of war and counter-revolution, which explains why 'revolutionary Jacobinism preached the virtues of representative institutions and practiced the rigors of revolutionary government'.[10]

What the Jacobins did possess, and the Girondins did not, however, was an unparalled network of clubs, radiating from the *'le club-mère'* in Paris to every corner of France, as well as to some of the major European cities. Michael Kennedy estimates that around 2 per cent of the French population was caught up in the Jacobin net, covering, as early as 1791, over 400 clubs.[11] During the Terror, Jacobinism could create an alternative, 'unofficial' and revolutionary structure of government, headed by the *représentants-en-mission*, functioning through the Jacobin provincial clubs and operating alongside the thousands of *comités de surveillance* created in March by the Convention. At the apex of this 'Revolutionary Government of the Year II' were the two great committees – the Committee of General Security, whose main jurisdiction was confined to police affairs, and the far more influential Committee of Public Safety, whose brief extended to every other aspect of government, military and civil. It must be remembered that the latter committee, composed of twelve deputies, including the 'triumvirate', Robespierre, Couthon and Saint-Just, as well as very influential figures like Carnot (in charge of military affairs) and Lindet (food supplies), was created by, and was ultimately responsible to, the National Convention. Robespierre would be overthrown inside, not outside, the Convention.

The second major prop upon which the Jacobin Government of the Year II rested was the Popular Movement, particularly in Paris. It was a movement, unlike typical eighteenth-century 'crowds', which was organised and, even more important, armed. During the critical period of the summer of 1793 to the spring of the following year, the sansculottes, meeting nightly in draughty 'nationalised' church halls draped with the appropriate revolutionary symbolism of tricolour flags, extracts from the Declaration of the Rights of Man, 'busts of the martyrs', injected more revolutionary and martial vigour into the Republic's struggle for existence than any other socio-political group in the country. The forty-eight Sections of the capital – provincial towns had also been divided into Sections, originally for electoral and administrative purposes – had been transformed, following their invasion by 'passive' citizens in the summer of 1792, into engines of political activity. Each Section had its own officials and committees, including the powerful *comités de surveillance*; each of them sent two representatives to sit on the Paris Commune. Not all of the Sections were radical; indeed, it was not until the autumn of 1793 that the radical Sections came to dominate the capital. The sansculottes, as these political activists proudly called themselves, took the Constitution of 1793 seriously. Whether or not their political programme, which included the 'sovereignty of the people' and the 'sacred right of insurrection', sprang from hand-me-down versions of Rousseau or the requirements of a depressed artisanal and shopkeeper society (something we shall discuss in more detail in chapter five), they came into increasing conflict with a Jacobin Government which had a country to run and two major wars, civil and foreign, to win.

The Jacobin system of government, always intended as temporary, was forged in the white heat of revolution and war, tempered by the internecine feuds within the Convention and the Paris Commune, and packaged in a Rousseauesque wrapping of civic and political *vertu*. The feuds within the Convention were provoked by the overall strategy of the Committee of Public Safety which sought, initially, to harness the popular fury of the sansculottes against the enemies of the Republic, and then, when success beckoned, to rein it in, a move prompted by the increasing fears of the propertied elites. By the autumn of 1793, a period often described as the 'anarchic period of the Terror', the Parisian sansculottes had completed their defeat of the moderates in the Parisian Sections and had launched a successful invasion of the National Convention (4–5 September) which, reluctantly, granted them legislation aimed at fixing the price of basic commodities (the Law of the General Maximum) and the creation of a 'Revolutionary Army', destined to become the striking force of the Terror in the provinces. The forty or so *armées révolutionnaires* totalling some 40,000 volunteer ex-soldiers, artisans and craftsmen and spearheaded by the Parisian *armée* led by Ronsin, provided the necessary sanction of force. Without it, the sansculottes argued, peasants and merchants would not empty their barns and warehouses of goods, especially if they were obliged to take the increasingly worthless *assignats* as payment. More than any other single factor, it was these *armées* which drove the Republic to the edge of anarchy during the autumn and winter months of 1793–4, as they marched from their urban bases out into the countryside to sell the message of the sansculotte Revolution, more often than not to a bewildered, even hostile countryside. As Richard Cobb put it, the *armées*, for all the brevity of their existence,

> were 'essential cogs in the administration of the Terror; they represented the Terror on the move, the village Terror'. The *armées* came closest to realizing the dream of every sectionary militant – a guillotine on wheels, casting its long shadow over grain hoarders, counter-revolutionary priests, and foreign spies.[12]

The *armées révolutionnaires*, however, represented just one agency among several that brought the Revolution into the kitchens of most Frenchmen, if only briefly, in that memorable Year II of the Revolution. There were also the *représentants-en-mission* who were despatched to every department, or groups of departments in 1793, acting as the political and judicial lords and masters of all they surveyed, purging and energising the local popular societies and *comités de surveillance*, organising the repression of counter-revolutionary forces in cities like Nantes and Lyon, where *représentants* Carrier in the former city and Fouché and Collot d'Herbois in the latter carried the responsibility, along with detachments of the *armées révolutionnaires*, for the barbaric killings of several thousand opponents of the Revolution. *Représentants, armées révolutionnaires*, and the *comités de surveillance* were also the main agencies behind that brief spasm of dechristianisation which swept parts of France in the autumn of 1793. *Représentant* Fouché had sparked things off with the closure of churches in the Nièvre department, his action being imitated by Chaumette in Paris where, early in November, God was ejected from the cathedral of Notre-Dame in favour of the Goddess of Reason. Many of the Parisian Sections eagerly joined the priest-hunt. In the Gravilliers, Jacques Roux's Section, a seven-year-old boy, whose father had been killed at the front, was brought to the lectern to announce the closure of all the Section's churches, describing them as 'these lairs frequented by ravenous animals which devour the people's daily bread'.[13] In the provinces, *représentant* Javogues issued a decree on 1 *nivôse* Year II/21 December 1793 which converted all the churches of the department of the Loire into Temples of Reason. One rationale behind Javogues' action, as indeed behind many acts of dechristianisation in late 1793 was the need to seize church gold and silver for the war effort.[14] After 1792, but particularly during the Year II, Mars was the deity who actually presided over the actions of most Frenchmen and women.

The revolutionary energies released by engaging at least the sympathetic sections of the population in the struggle did produce the desired results, at home and abroad. The *levée-en-masse*, decreed by the Convention on 23 August 1793 would enable the Minister of War to command around a million men by the end of the year, a force which would ultimately decide the fortunes of the Revolution. Nevertheless, it was the popular enthusiasm to save France from the foreigner and the Revolution from his agents inside France which prompted so many to join the tricolours. If the Revolution was not exactly a welcome visitor in every home, the counter-revolution, as opposed to apathetic or sporadic resistance to the Revolution, remained the choice of a minority, albeit a very dedicated one. In the Vendée, the ebb-tide of counter-revolution was clearly discernible after the defeat of the *armée catholique* at Cholet on 17–18 October; a week or so earlier, the city of Lyon, whose loss to the counter-revolution in the summer had represented a serious blow to the credibility of the Republic, was retaken by revolutionary forces. Thousands of its inhabitants were to be guillotined or shot in the retributive reaction which ensued; hundreds of priests would be drowned in the river Loire by Carrier based at Nantes, the other focal point for the provincial counter-revolution. At the front, the victories over the British at Hondschoote, near Dunkirk, on 8 September and over the Austrians at the battle of Wattignies five weeks later relieved the threat of invasion from the north whilst, in the south, the far weaker Spanish threat was parried and then repulsed.

Gradually, the political and military circumstances for reining in the forces unleashed by mass popular involvement in the Revolution were being created. It is important to stress that Robespierre and the majority of his colleagues had always been uneasy about the more extreme members and policies of the Popular Movement: Robespierre was not the type of man who enjoyed a 'night with the boys' in the working-class *cabarets* of the faubourg Saint-Marcel: Danton, of course, would have been quite keen. The process of political disengagement from the Popular Movement may be said to have begun as early as August with Robespierre's denunciation of the *Enragé* leader, Jacques Roux, who did know how the less fortunate members of society actually lived. On 9 September – just four days after the invasion of the Convention by the sansculottes it should be noted – the Parisian Sections were denied the right to sit *en permanence*. The sansculottes would trump this move by setting up their own popular societies in each Section (the *sociétés sectionnaires*), underlining the fact that the Jacobin Government was still too weak to impose its will unchallenged. It could, however, strike at the women's movement which received scant support from the male chauvinist sansculottes. At the end of October, all clubs set up by women were closed, ending a very interesting and dangerous link between a putative form of feminism and the political extremism of the *Enragés*. It could also strike against common enemies: in the same month, Marie Antoinette and the leading Girondist deputies were executed.

The 'Triumvirate' of Robespierre, Couthon and Saint-Just experienced far more difficulty mastering the forces of opposition to the CPS based in the Convention and the Paris Commune. Apart from a clutch of deputies tainted by corruption or links with foreign governments, there were two important factions opposing the Jacobin Government during the winter of 1793-94 – the moderates in the Convention grouped around Georges Danton and Camille Desmoulins, and the extremists led by Hébert and Chaumette with their power base in the Paris Commune. The former should not be dismissed as unprincipled seekers after money and power: the Dantonists stood for an end to the Terror and a possible peace with Britain, representing a strand of opinion which links them to the Girondins. The Hébertists, on the other hand, represented that uncompromising call to arms on the part of the Popular Movement; increased Terror to defeat the foreigner abroad allied, and this is the important point, to a social policy directed at the 'selfish rich' at home. Throughout the month of November, Robespierre moved cautiously, denouncing extremism in all its forms, purging the Jacobin Club of 'foreign' plotters, particularly those involved in the dechristianisation campaign. During this period, Robespierre was the epitome of the careful politician, 'the government man, who sees no difference between right and left, between *ultras* and *citras* as they were called: he saw only disequilibrium, crisis and competitors'.[15]

It was the passing of the decree of 14 *frimaire* Year II/4 December 1793 which clearly marks the swing of the political pendulum away from an alliance with the Popular Movement towards the creation of a strong, centralised, bureaucratic State. It was the weapon which would enable the Robespierrists to resolve the social and political conflicts which were threatening to strangle the infant Republic. The excesses of the Popular Movement would be ended, redirected into goals assigned by the Revolutionary Government. But, there was a bill to pay. The decree of 14 *frimaire* brought all government bodies, administrative and police, under the direct control of the two great Committees; it made the district, not the department, the basic unit of administration; it created the *agent national*, obliged to report to Paris every ten days; it forbade popular societies, indeed any political or administrative body, from communicating with each other. The decree represents a milestone in the history of the centralised French State; the *agent national* takes his modest place in the line of centralising French officials from the *ancien régime* Intendant to the present-day Prefect.

However, instead of being the first stage in the dismantling of the Terror, the spring of 1794 would see the start of the 'Great Terror'. More people – over 1,500 – would be executed at the hands of the Revolutionary Tribunal from March to August 1794 than had been executed during the previous year. Amongst its more famous victims would be the Dantonists and the Hébertists; both factions perceived the dangers of the increasing 'dictatorship' of Robespierre and the Committee of Public Safety, both were foolhardy, or brave, enough to imagine that they were immune from its consequences. Hébert and his supporters went to the guillotine on 4 *germinal*/24 March; Danton and his friends were executed just under a fortnight later. Why was the Revolution 'beginning to devour its own'? François Furet refuses to accept the line that we must continue to link Terror to war and counter-revolution, and, given that Westermann had finally crushed the Vendéeans at the bloody battle of Savenay on 23 December 1793 and that, by the summer of 1794, the regular army would be moving beyond France's frontiers to 'liberate' the Low Countries, Catalonia and Italy, there is clearly merit in his argument. Reflecting the main thrust of recent revisionist thinking on the Revolution, Furet prefers an 'idealist' interpretation: the 'Robespierrist clan', in particular, was seeking nothing less than the 'regeneration of man', the creation, in fact, of a new man, *political* man, capable of solving all problems through political processes. The Terror went on because defeat over the enemies of the Revolution marked but the first stage in this process of regeneration and rebirth whose roots lay in the eighteenth-century Enlightenment.[16] Albert Soboul, adopting a more social approach, argues that in the final analysis the Revolutionary Government was being undermined by the fact that it did not 'rest on a solid class basis'. However, he also notes that the increasing powers of the State 'paralysed the critical spirit and political militancy which had previously characterized the Parisian masses'.[17] We shall examine the issue of the political and cultural 'regeneration' of revolutionary man in some detail in our final chapter.

What is not in doubt is the marked expansion of the centralised, bureaucratic State. John Bosher, in his recent textbook on the Revolution, offers chapter and verse for this extremely important development.[18] From the spring of 1794, the Committee of Public Safety began to drive this increasingly powerful State machine with far less regard for those who got in its way. Confronted with its advance, the sansculottes 'voluntarily' shut down their societies in the Sections; in April, the CPS created its own *bureau de police*, provoking increased enmity from the Committee of General Security; on 22 *prairial*/ 10 June, the infamous law which stripped accused persons of any serious defence rights was passed, accelerating the work of the Revolutionary Tribunal. Two days earlier, reflecting his own strongly deist belief and the need to bind the divided nation together within one spiritual framework, Robespierre had headed the great procession in Paris to celebrate the Feast of the Supreme Being. God was back in his heaven – or rather Rousseau's! – and all was well with Robespierre's world. If political unity amongst French men and women could not be achieved in this world, perhaps it might be possible in the next! L'Incorruptible had begun to lose touch with political reality. As Barère struggled to bring warring factions within the two great Committees together and some of the old *représentants-en-mission*, such as Fouché and Tallien, plotted to escape the fate of fellow-deputies like Danton, Robespierre, during these critical times, even absented himself from the meetings of the Committee of Public Safety. His famous speech on 8 *thermidor*, denouncing 'enemies of the State,' provoked the *coup* within the Convention that toppled him and his supporters the following day. Repressed and depressed, the sansculottes failed to muster the necessary support to save them. Robespierre and over seventy of his supporters would be executed in the immediate aftermath of the *coup*.

From July 1794 to the advent of the Directory in September 1795 – the period known as the Thermidorean regime – attempts were made, yet again, to 'terminer la Révolution'. According to William Doyle, 'The ninth of Thermidor marked not so much the overthrow of one man or group of men as the rejection of a form of government.'[19] However, as Danton and others had realised, ending the Revolution was inextricably linked to ending the war, and that was hardly a practical proposition, first because, as the royalist Declaration of Verona on 24 June 1795 made abundantly clear, the exiled monarchy would not recognise the gains, particularly of clerical and *émigré* lands, acquired by the revolutionary elites; and second because the war was about to enter its most favourable phase for the French, as Russia, Prussia and Austria, turned their attentions to the far easier task of dismembering Poland. The immediate task confronting the Thermidoreans, therefore, was the completion of the work begun by the Robespierrists after the spring of 1794 – emasculating the political powers of the Popular Movement. The Thermidoreans actually did what the more elitist leaders of the Revolution, such as Mounier or Mirabeau, had longed to do in 1789 – crush the monster of 'popular despotism'. Much, though certainly not all, of the legislation of the Year II would be repealed: the Terror would be relaxed, some measure of decentralisation introduced, but the Revolution would continue, albeit in a far more elitist form. Physically weakened by the demands of five years of Revolution, exhausted by the purge of militants in the Sections and the strains of the icy winter of 1794–5, the Parisian Popular Movement would be dealt a mortal blow after the two popular uprisings of *germinal* and *prairial* Year III (1 April and 20 May 1795). Having dealt with the threat from the left, the Thermidoreans agreed to devise a constitution which would not only secure the perpetuation of their political powers, but would effectively exclude the masses from power. The constitutional settlement of the late 1790s would represent a significant move towards the English model, just as the right wing of the National Assembly in 1789 had wanted. An executive of five Directors, a bicameral legislature – a Council of 500 and a Council of Elders – and, most significant of all, the reduction of the electorate, in practice if not in theory, to fewer than 40,000. This made the much-debated division of the electorate between 'active' and 'passive' citizens introduced by the Constitution of 1791 appear extremely radical, but then a lot of blood, too much of it bourgeois, had flowed under the revolutionary bridge since then.

After 1795, the energies of the French people would be diverted abroad, as the regime laid the foundations of the Napoleonic Empire, creating puppet states in the Low Countries, Switzerland and Italy. Tim Blanning makes an interesting point when he links the continuation and extension of war after 1795 to the return of surviving Girondins, prepared to take on 'the rest of the Continent with reckless abandon'.[20] It is an interesting point: on the social plane also, the Girondins were prepared to be far harsher in implementing the social policies of the possessing class. These were the surviving Girondins, after all, politicians who had learned one thing above all from the Terror, and the execution of so many of their friends – there was, henceforth, to be no supping with the sansculotte devil. Many would applaud the wave of violence known as the White Terror which was directed at former terrorists during the spring and summer of 1795 affecting, in particular, some of the royalist/federalist strongholds like Lyon, Nîmes and Marseille. Grisly and macabre imitations of the September Massacres of 1792 would be re-enacted in the prisons of these troubled cities.

Little wonder that when opposition from the left resurfaced in 1796, it would do so in a very different form, that of Babouvism. Gracchus Babeuf, often referred to as 'the first communist', was a militant who had lived the Revolution, first as a minor Jacobin administrator, then as the editor of a newspaper, *Le Tribun du Peuple*, and, finally, as the leader of the 'Conspiracy of the Equals' which was formed in the spring of 1796. His ideas, linked tenuously to Enlightenment thought, were shaped in the main by the tragic experience of the Popular Movement during the Terror, prompting Babeuf and his handful of followers to re-assess the tactics of popular revolution. On one level, Babouvism was the Popular Movement's response to the crisis of the developing bourgeois State, deformed by war, as well as to the exclusion of the people from the political scene. As his biographer notes, Babeuf had been a progressive democrat in 1793, only to be disillusioned by the repressive actions of Robespierre and his Thermidorean successors. In 1796, Babeuf and his supporters would construct a centralised, elitist programme of revolution, complete with a temporary (three months!) dictatorship on behalf of the people. Links with Lenin and the Bolsheviks are obvious, if misleading.[21] Reflecting the militarisation of French politics and society by 1795, it is interesting that Babeuf forged closer links with the army and the police than with the popular militants in the Sections, but then many of the latter, of course, were still in prison. After 19 *fructidor* Year VI/ 5 September 1798, the Jourdan Law, the first modern conscription law, would redirect the energies of youth towards the battlefields of Europe: democratic participation would subsequently be channelled 'far more into the military affairs of the French nation than into its patterns of domestic politics and administration'.[22]

The popular counter-revolution had been forced into military uniform, almost from the beginning. Following the crushing military defeats in December 1793, bands of Catholic royalist guerillas called *chouans*, 'overwhelmingly plebeian' in social composition, had regrouped in Brittany, emerging by the spring of 1794 as 'an effective military force'. In the south-east, Catholic royalist *égorgeurs*, who had first tasted blood during the White Terror of the spring and summer of 1795, would organise in loose guerilla bands to terrorise local populations well into the reign of Napoleon Bonaparte. In the west and the south-east, recruits to these bands were, more often than not, young men evading the increasingly draconian conscription laws of the Revolution.[23]

Under the Directory, the political system itself would become a pawn of ambitious generals, particularly Hoche and Napoleon, the latter, by 1797, already signing treaties with foreign governments. Only a series of *coups d'état* kept the fairly corrupt system going. The first, on 13 *vendémiaire* Year IV/5 October 1795, had repressed a disjointed royalist uprising in Paris organised to protest against the 'Law of the Two-Thirds' which secured the re-election of two-thirds of the deputies already sitting in the National Convention. The royalist threat refused to go away; indeed, royalists of various hues secured a majority in the elections of 1797, provoking the second *coup* on 18 *fructidor* Year V/4 September 1797 which annulled the election of 177 deputies suspected of royalist sympathies. These were good days for the Directory, a mortal blow dealt to the royalist right following upon considerable success abroad, highlighted by the Treaty of Campio Formio with Austria on 27 *vendémiaire* Year VI/18 October 1797 which led to the recognition of the new satellite republics created by the French in the Low Countries, Germany and Italy. The third *coup*, on 22 *floréal* Year VI/11 May 1798, was launched to prevent a Jacobin renaissance; the final *coup* on 18 *brumaire* Year VIII/9 November 1799 would bring Napoleon Bonaparte to power. It is relevant to note here that, from the autumn of 1798, Russia, Austria and England had formed a Second Coalition which explains the deteriorating military situation, the external backcloth to Napoleon's seizure of power. Internally, politics at local level by 1799 had become a battle for survival, as Jacobins and Royalists killed each other outside polling stations. Isser Woloch states that the *commissaires de la République*, created by the Directory to link the administrative periphery with the centre, never recovered their commitment after the 'near-anarchy and anti-republican violence that engulfed certain departments in 1796';[24] Malcolm Crook, whilst acknowledging the contribution of the Revolution towards the 'longer-term process of political acculturation', offers a convincing analysis of the declining graph of political participation by the late 1790s, set, as it should be, within 'a context of war and civil war'.[25]

After 1795, the French Revolution continued, but wearing a military uniform and without the active support of the masses. In 1799, that master constitution-maker the *abbé* Sieyès was called upon once again to produce a dish fit for the new, surrogate king, Napoleon Bonaparte. His idea of a 'Great Elector' (based presumably on Rousseau's 'Legislator') was an abortive attempt to find that replacement for Louis XVI which had eluded the early leaders of the Revolution. There was to be no surrogate for the masses, French liberalism had emerged from the Revolution in very conservative garb: 'from the time of the Jacobin dictatorship onwards he [Sieyès] felt the need not merely to construct a system of government that incorporated the basic principles of the Revolution, but at the same time to protect such a structure against overthrow by either demagogic or reactionary forces'.[26] It is difficult to find a more appropriate comment on the nature of the fragile and conservative form of liberalism that emerged in France from the traumas of the Revolution.

Part II

4 The political economy of the Revolution

The French Revolution was born and died in a state of bankruptcy: on 16 August 1788, the royal government suspended interest payments to its creditors, revealing, in effect, that it was bankrupt; on 9 *vendémiaire* Year VI/30 September 1797, a republican government arbitrarily wiped out two-thirds of the debt it owed its creditors. There is a strong case for arguing that the Directorial regime, like its royal predecessor, never recovered from the ensuing loss of public confidence. In recent years, a few historians have condemned the Revolution, from start to finish, as 'a national catastrophe', whilst others, chanting monetarist and free-market themes, have joined in the denunciatory chorus.[1] Certainly the conflict between those who advocated free-trade approaches to the economy and those who favoured a more traditonal system of regulations and controls lies at the heart of the economic history of the Revolution; but it is also central to an understanding of the economic history of the *ancien régime*, particularly during its final decades when royal policies oscillated between the two extremes. Pressure from consumers, especially for bread, forced governments to modify or abandon free-trade policies before and during the Revolution. Unlike royal ministers before 1789, however, the leaders of the Revolution were confronted, after 1792, with a state of total war. Once again, we are reminded of the importance of war in determining the course of the Revolution. As François Hincker remarks: 'There can be no doubt that it was the war, to be more precise, the formation of the Grand Coalition against the French in February 1793, which represents the crucial date so far as the economic history of the Revolution is concerned.'[2]

Some revisionist historians, anxious to lay the responsibility for the economic failures of the 1790s firmly at the feet of the 'Jacobin controlled economy', suggest that the French economy was flourishing on the eve of the Revolution. In his best-selling work, *Citizens*, the

storian Simon Schama wrote this: 'on the eve of the
he trajectory was pointing sharply upwards'.[3] In fact, in
l sectors of the economy, the opposite was true. William
ting to the periodic slumps in the production of grain and
g the period 1770 to 1789, concludes that 'because
agricultu.. was far away the most important economic activity in the
kingdom, the shock waves were felt throughout economic life'. This,
Doyle continues, had an adverse effect in the industrial sector, making
the reign of Louis XVI 'an uncertain time in industrial as well as
agricultural terms. The silk industry lurched from crisis to crisis.
Markets for woollens and linens became extremely erratic. Only
cottons continued the sustained expansion that all textiles had
experienced in mid-century.'[4] My own work on the economy of Lower
Languedoc confirms this pessimistic analysis.

Let us put some statistical flesh on the bones of these arguments. It
is generally agreed that agricultural production rose by 30–40 per cent
between 1700 and 1790; wheat by around 60 per cent between the
1730s and the 1780s, rye by 60–71 per cent.[5] In the industrial sector,
whilst there was an average annual rise of only 1 per cent in the
woollen industry during the eighteenth century, growth in other
important areas of the economy produced significantly higher rates –
cotton 1.9 per cent, cast-iron and coal almost 4 per cent per annum.[6]
In a few regions, obvious signs of an 'industrial revolution' were
discernible. In and around Mulhouse, for example, the production of
printed cotton fabrics (*indiennes*) increased, between 1758 and 1784,
by over 700 per cent; the Anzin coal-mines in northern France had
become the most productive on the continent by 1789. Cristophe
Oberkampf's cotton products made at Jouy-en-Josas were gaining
international repute; four years before the Revolution, 4,000 workers
were being employed at the Sazet spinning factory in Nantes; in the
heavy industrial sector, Ignace de Wendel was experimenting with
coke-fired furnaces at le Creusot, whilst, at Chaillot near Paris, the
Périer brothers were making their first steam-engines.[7] Industrial
oases in an agricultural desert perhaps, but we need to remind
ourselves that the Industrial Revolution in Britain spread from a few
specialised regions – South Wales, Lanarkshire, the West Riding, the
Black Country, the mill-towns of Lancashire.

However, as we saw in our opening chapter, it was foreign and
colonial trade which provided the best testimony to the unquestioned
rise of France as a leading economic power on the world stage, the
vitality of this sector encouraging the growth of internal trade along
the river networks of the Garonne, the Seine and the Rhône. During

the course of the eighteenth century, total foreign trade quadrupled, trade with Europe trebled, whereas trade with France's colonies increased tenfold. It has been estimated that, on the eve of the Revolution, France imported from her colonies – of which Saint-Domingue represented the jewel in the French crown – 134 million *livres*' worth of sugar and coffee, 26 million *livres*' worth of raw cotton, 10 million *livres*' worth of cocoa beans and ginger.[8] In return, French shippers and merchants made, and lost, their fortunes in the slave trade, exporting manufactured and food products to the colonies, and re-exporting colonial goods to England and other countries on the continent. Perhaps as much as a quarter of France's foreign trade consisted of re-exports. Once again, however, we should note that the percentage of manufactured goods, relative to total colonial exports, was dropping by the 1780s.

This last point serves as a reminder that, from the standpoint of France's domestic economy, excluding the growth industries of cotton, coal and iron which made a relatively small contribution to France's gross national product (coal production, for example, was still well under a million *tonnes* a year on the eve of the Revolution), all was definitely not well. The boom decades of the French economy from the 1730s to the 1770s had been founded upon luxury goods, the textile industry – mainly woollens and linens – wines and brandies; during the reign of Louis XVI, periodic crises eroded the base of the old prosperity. The textile industries of Brittany and Normandy in the west, the Languedoc silk and woollen industries in the south were in slow, but terminal decline long before the Revolution. The famous silk industry in and around the city of Nîmes in south-eastern France, which had started with 1,000 looms producing silk stockings in 1740, provided work for 6,000 looms by the 1770s, only half of which were working on the eve of the Revolution.[9] The 'âge d'or' of the Languedoc textile industry had ended before the 1780s, not the 1790s; the same is true of the textile industries in many regions of western France. In Troyes, the value of textile goods produced halved in the latter part of the 1780s. As for the wine industry, the 1780s proved to be a decade of crisis, a consequence of bad harvests and over-production.

The explanation for the crisis affecting the French economy during the reign of Louis XVI may be divided into the contingent and the structural. There was the closure of American markets during the War of Independence from 1778 to 1783; the fact that France was becoming uncompetitive as other countries modernised their economies; the closure of the Spanish and South American markets after 1778. In 1786, the free-trade Eden Treaty with England, which facilitated the entry of English textile goods, came at a most inopportune time, given the crisis already afflicting certain sectors of the French textile industry. Finally, there were the bad harvests of 1787 and 1788 which drove the poor to the brink of starvation and which seriously affected the manufacturing sector since the majority of the population ceased to buy manufactured goods. Had it not been for the agricultural crisis, the government of Louis XVI might have weathered, for a time anyway, the social crisis and ensuing political storm. But, within a couple of years, the government had been forced back on to the traditional policies of intervention. The old cycle revolved again, as it was to do throughout the 1790s and, in some measure, to the present day in capitalist societies.

But the crisis of 1787–9, which certainly helps to explain the timing of the outbreak of revolution, was also related to deeper, more long-term, structural weaknesses, both political and economic. The fact was the Bourbons were trying, haphazardly, to develop a modern State and a modern economy upon the bases of a traditional, hierarchical society, albeit one undergoing significant changes. Political struggles at Court, between Turgot and his enemies in the 1770s or between Calonne and his enemies a decade later, were related to this fundamental problem. A modern State presupposed a modern taxation system which France manifestly lacked. The persistence of feudal social structures meant that the real wealth of the country was not taxed: the great landowners, the Church and the nobility, escaped most of the taxes which fell upon land. The banking, merchant and manufacturing class benefited from the absence of any real pay-as-you-earn scheme, so that the main burden of taxation fell upon those who could least afford it – the landowning peasantry. And not only did the latter have to pay increasingly onerous direct government taxes, like the *taille*, but they were also forced to pay heavy indirect taxes on salt (the hated *gabelle*), drink (the *aides*) and tobacco, *after* they had paid their tithe (the *dîme*) to the church and their feudal dues to their *seigneurs*. The provincial assembly of Upper Guyenne put it very succinctly: 'out of a dozen sheaves of corn, the seigneur takes three, the tithe owner one, while (government) taxes absorb two more'.[10]

Of course, the more far-sighted government ministers, such as Turgot and Calonne, knew what had to be done – introduce a more equitable land tax, which is what they tried and failed to do from 1774 to 1789. It was the Revolution which dealt the death-blow to privilege, on that famous night of 4 August 1789 when privilege and particularism were uprooted in one delirious night of political passion. As

Georges Lefebvre wrote: 'the essential work of the Revolution of 1789 may be found registered in the resolutions of the 4 August and in the Declaration of the Rights of Man and the Citizen'.[11] One cannot overestimate the importance of the abolition of feudalism. Although it took four years to effect in law and much longer in the minds of the French people, it cleared the ground for a completely new taxation system, one that would fall, rather more equitably at least, on rich and poor alike.

But, in 1789, the new revolutionary government was still bankrupt, and something had to be done urgently if the Revolution was to survive at all. In June 1789, the Third Estate had decreed that all *ancien régime* taxes were illegal, leaving the Constituent Assembly to introduce a completely new tax system, founded upon (i) a land tax (*contribution foncière*), (ii) a poll or personal tax (*contribution mobilière et personelle*), and, representing at least a first move towards taxing the manufacturing class, (iii) the *patente* tax (payable on setting up a business). Indirect taxes, like those on drink and salt, were abolished from 1789 to 1796. But the responsibility for assessing and levying the new taxes fell upon the local municipalities, and, in some cases, it was not until 1792 that the new system was truly operative. Income from the land tax for 1791 was 34 million *livres* instead of the 300 million the government had anticipated.[12] Meanwhile, bills and creditors would have to be paid. To plug this massive gap, the Constituent Assembly took the most fateful decision of its life – the seizure of two billion *livres'* worth of Church lands, decreed by the Constituent Assembly on 2 November 1789. This move, and the linked new religious settlement, the Civil Constitution of the Clergy (12 July 1790), produced a seismic fault in the political geology of the French Revolution, provoking repeated tremors throughout every section of French society, down to Napoleon's Concordat with the Papacy in 1801. The sale of 'National Lands' – as confiscated Church property was now described – represents the most important revolution, from an economic, social and religious standpoint, within the French Revolution. It serves to remind us that money, if not monetarism, *was* at the root of many of the evils which beset the leaders of the Revolution; furthermore, that it was the introduction of paper money called *assignats* which eventually posed insoluble problems for every administration from 1789 to 1796, when they were abolished. Why?

Primarily because, instead of limiting their use to paying off the State's debts by exchanging them for Church and, subsequently, *émigré* property, successive administrations decided to use them to finance the costs of war and the rebuilding of the French State. The original intention was that the State's creditors would be paid off in *assignats* which they would then exchange for National Lands – the *assignats* would then return to the specially created *Caisse de l'Extraordinaire* to be destroyed. A neat solution, and, for a time it seemed to work. Confidence in the *assignat* remained high until the beginning of 1792, but thereafter it dropped sharply, with periods of stabilisation, particularly during the Jacobin Terror. The explanation for its fall is not difficult to ascertain. During the first year, only 1,200 million *livres'* worth of *assignats* had been printed, representing, possibly, around a third of the actual value of the Church lands which had been seized. Between September 1790 and May 1792, only an additional 100 million *livres'* worth of *assignats* were issued. Thereafter, increasing emission of notes, way beyond the value of the land upon which their security rested, led to decreasing confidence and increasing inflation. Although a 100-*livre assignat* note rose from just over 20 per cent of its face-value in August 1793 to almost 50 per cent by the end of the year, it dropped sharply thereafter as the cost of war imposed new demands on the Revolutionary Government. By 1795, *assignats* to the value of no less than 19 billion *livres* had been printed; by the time of their abolition, in February 1796, when a 100-*livre* note was not worth the paper it was printed on, this figure had almost doubled. The scale of the disaster for those good revolutionaries who had dealt only in *assignats* may be judged from the fact that if one had been silly enough to hold on to *assignats* worth 3,000 *livres* in 1790, he or she would have received just one *livre* in hard cash for them by 1796! On the other hand, as Balzac was to chronicle a few decades after the Revolution, fortunes were made by those who speculated in the *assignat* as well as by those who bought land or who paid off their State and private debts in increasingly worthless paper money. The greatest fortunes in land were accumulated during the brief few months in 1796 when the Directory introduced a hare-brained scheme to convert – at a rate of 1 to 30 – *assignats* into what were called *mandats territoriaux*. The *assignat* experiment lasted six years; the *mandats* just six months. The experiment with paper money during the Revolution unquestionably increased the profound suspicion, dating from the collapse of John Law's financial schemes at the beginning of the century, with which the general public in France viewed State-guaranteed paper money, with important consequences for the development of capitalism in the nineteenth century.

Almost all economic historians agree on this, but on little else. Florin Aftalion, relying heavily on recent monetarist theories, believes that the massive inflation associated with the *assignat* and the sale of National Lands offers 'a perfectly satisfactory explanation as to why the French Revolution, which was undertaken in order to put an end to "tyranny" and to establish a just society, degenerated into looting, Terror and dictatorship'.[13] François Hincker, on the other hand, having pointed out that an increase in the money supply was not exactly unknown under the *ancien régime*, provides a more balanced assessment, concluding that 'when attributing responsibility for the disorganisation of production and exchange between 1793 and 1797, it is impossible to isolate monetary factors, particularly since France was in the midst of total war and social demands were exacerbated'. He also notes that the wild inflationary, then deflationary cycle of the 1790s fulfilled the aim of the authors of the *assignat* experiment, which was to wipe out the State's debt. Even *before* the State arbitrarily reduced its debt by two-thirds on 9 *vendémiaire* Year VI/30 September 1797, the national debt had been reduced to just 7 per cent of its total budget. In 1789, it had represented 250 per cent![14] Clearly this 'success' was bought at an immense price. Is it too much to suggest that this price might have been the French bourgeoisie's belief in parliamentary government? The political economy of the Revolution was founded upon the nervous reactions of a bourgeoisie paralysed by war, civil war and rampant inflation. In these circumstances a country seat was far more valuable than a seat in parliament!

Denied substantial investment at home the Directory by 1797 was balancing the books through a policy of taxing and looting conquered territories: by March of that year, the Treasury had received around 50 million *livres* in hard cash from Napoleon's Army of Italy, and that was only the beginning of this bounty from the 'sister republics' conquered by the French. Here we arrive at the crucial intersection of war and finance: a great deal has been written about war, far less about the men and the financial system which propped up the Revolution, at least not since John Bosher's pioneering work on the subject a generation ago which stressed the role of finance in the creation of the modern, bureaucratic French State.[15] Recently, however, historians have taken up where Bosher left off. Let us illustrate this point by looking very briefly at two major figures – Paul-Joseph Cambon and Dominique-Vincent Ramel: the former was in charge of finance throughout the period of the National Convention; the latter's official career covers almost the whole of the Directory, from February 1796 to July 1799. Henri Guillemin, in his study of Robespierre, reminds us that Cambon played a starring role in the drama of 9 *thermidor* Year II/27 July 1794. Robespierre, in the course of his fatal last speeech to the National Convention on 26 July 1794 included a bitter attack on Cambon, accused of having 'encouraged [through the uncontrolled emission of *assignats*] speculation', and of favouring wealthy creditors at the expense of the poor who had been driven 'to ruin and despair'.[16] Michel Brugière's detailed study of those who ran, and those who profited from, the Revolution, allows us to place the spotlight on the career of Dominique-Vincent Ramel, whose contribution was more positive than that of Cambon. It was Ramel who master-minded in 1796 the return to hard currency and the creation of the *Agence des contributions directes*, thus laying the foundations for a modern tax-collection system in France; whose scheming with private financiers and the Treasury formed an important backcloth – again often overlooked – in the *coup d'état* of 18 *fructidor* Year V/4 September 1797; who organised the financial epilogue to the French Revolution, the 'Bankruptcy of the Two-Thirds' three weeks later. Finally, it was Ramel who privatised many of the State's activities, negotiating massive contracts, increasingly after 1798, with influential bankers and army contractors such as Gabriel-Julien Ouvrard who was to amass an immense personal fortune. By the time Napoleon came to power in November 1799, the French State had been restructured around the loot imported by generals (amounting, possibly, to a quarter of total revenues) and the activities of bankers and army contractors who organised and financed the military show. The political economy of the Revolution had been transformed into a war economy.[17]

Following the arrest and execution of the Robespierrists, ministers like Cambon joined in the national political game of *sauve qui peut*, denouncing the 'economic terrorism' of the Year II which he had run so effectively (it did him little good in the long run, for he was forced to flee in April 1795). Cambon's political pirouetting reminds us of the point we made at the beginning of this chapter – that the battle between the advocates of a controlled economy and those supporting more laissez-faire doctrines characterises the history of France, not just during, but before and after the Revolution, indeed, to the present day. In general terms, politicians, *Feuillant*, Girondin or Jacobin, and economic theorists like Dupont de Nemours, supported free-trade policies; popular 'public opinion' preferred the more traditional policies of regulations and controls. Again, in very general terms, the economic history of the period oscillates between free-trade periods from 1789 to late 1792 and from 1795 to 1799, with a patchy, controlled economy being introduced between 1792 and 1795 as a result of the pressures arising from war and the demands of consumers, urban and rural. De Nemours, who exercised considerable influence over the economic policies adopted during the early years of the Revolution, is typical of those politicians and intellectuals who had imbibed the physiocratic doctrines of free trade and (distinguishing the French physiocrats from the followers of Adam Smith) land as the source of all wealth. He had been at Turgot's side when that more famous son of physiocracy had introduced free trade in grain in 1775; he had helped to negotiate the Eden Treaty with England in 1786; and he had been at Calonne's side when the latter had re-introduced the freedom of the grain trade a year later.

Interesting that, on every occasion, the introduction of free-trade policies had led to mass popular resentment and resistance, which did not prevent de Dupont de Nemours from advocating the same policies in the whirlwind of revolutionary change from 1789 to 1792. Here again we see the direct influence of economic policy upon the political fortunes of the Revolution. From 1789 to 1792, the Constituent and Legislative Assemblies would try to implement the very programme that Turgot had failed to carry through from 1774 to 1776. Only a few days after it had decreed the political rights of man on 24 August 1789, the Constituent Assembly agreed to declare the economic rights of free-traders in grain. A year and a half later, it would, through the Allarde Law (2 March 1791), abolish the corporations which protected skilled craftsmen as well as privileges accorded to industry by the State. The important debate on the economy in the Legislative Assembly during the first week of December 1792 confirmed that, for the mainly wealthy revolutionary elite, economic and political freedoms were inseparable.

But already change was in the air, or rather in the fields and the streets, as popular pressure for a return to a more regulated economy, at least for basic foodstuffs, increased, a consequence of political uncertainty, poor-ish harvests and the combination of war and the economic consequences of the *assignat*. By the early spring of 1793, the National Convention was forced to accept petitions for a ceiling on price-rises from the sansculottes in the Parisian Sections as well as from the countryside, where, in the south-east, a mini-*Grande Peur* had broken out: 'insurgents responded to shortages and spiralling prices by intervening in the market-place to fix the price of grain'.[18] Traditional, popular self-defence mechanisms were operating, propelling Catholic–royalist movements forward, particularly in the Vendée. Not enough emphasis has been placed on the socio-economic consequences of the introduction of free-trade policies when explaining the rise of 'popular' counter-revolutionary movements. Initially, Girondins *and* Jacobins had reacted slowly, and very reluctantly, to popular pressure for a controlled economy: the former introduced the first, largely ineffective maximum on the price of grain on 4 May; the latter, the more famous and effective General Maximum on all basic foodstuffs on 29 September 1793, but only *after* an invasion of the Convention by the sansculottes.

The Girondins had created the machinery for the political *and* the economic terror of the Year II, but it was the Jacobins, as a result of their uneasy alliance with the popular movement, who made it work. The controlled economy of the Year II was not the manifestation of a coherent political philosophy of totalitarianism, certainly not that associated with twentieth-century communist regimes. Norman Hampson, no closet marxist, agrees. Even Saint-Just, for example, although not a 'pure economic liberal' (very few politicians were), believed that the State should only intervene in the economy 'in such a way that individuals, in pursuit of what they saw as their self-interest, would automatically contribute to the harmonious functioning of the system as a whole'. Hampson adds, however, that 'The gap between his theories and peasant ways of thinking was unbridgeable.'[19] That comment admirably sums up the chasm which separated the more ideological politician in the Revolution from the people who thought that 1789 had brought a new dawn, not the recurrence of old nightmares.

But if the Revolution was to be saved from counter-revolution and France itself from the Allied Powers then that chasm would have to be bridged: the 'controlled economy' of the Year II provided the necessary structure. It proved to be shaky and short-lived. The majority of Jacobins, Robespierre included, never really believed in it: they were no more 'interventionist' in economic affairs, from a theoretical standpoint, than they were 'totalitarian' in their political principles. Long before they fell from power, from December 1793 in fact, *after* the defeat of the Vendéean rebels, the Robespierrists had begun to distance themselves from the Popular Movement and begun to court the bankers and manufacturers upon whom, ultimately, the fate of the war depended. This shift of direction, towards greater freedom for profit-taking, may be discerned in the revisions to the General Maximum (3 *ventôse* Year II/21 February 1794) and the maximum of wages in Thermidor.

There certainly had been an attack upon 'the bastions of capitalism' at the height of the military and political crisis of the spring and summer of 1793, when the *Enragés* led by Jacques Roux, had been making the running – 11 April, all financial transactions to be conducted with *assignats*; 2 June, the closure of the Paris stock exchange; 24 August, the abolition of joint-stock societies. But this was a time when the Popular Movement was flexing its political muscle and the Committee of Public Safety had hardly got its act together. Absolute monarchy had consistently back-tracked from free-trade policies in periods of crisis; it is rather peculiar to blame the Jacobins for doing the same, particularly when one bears in mind the severity of the crisis. During the winter of 1793, the Popular Movement, using the threat of insurrection, forced the government to put teeth into the above legislation, primarily through the beloved, sansculotte *armées révolutionnaires* which as Richard Cobb has shown, were aimed at securing the circulation of foodstuffs, the supply of the urban markets, the observance of the General Maximum. The *armées révolutionnaires* were the teeth of the anti-capitalist Popular Movement, until they were drawn, let us recall, by Robespierre and his colleagues after only a few months.[20] But what of the famous 'Ventôse Decrees' (8–13 *ventôse*/26 February–3 March 1794) which, in theory at least since they were never really implemented, sought to distribute property confiscated from 'traitors'? Were they not evidence of the hidden 'socialist' intentions of the Robespierrists? Hardly: as Norman Hampson concludes, Saint-Just 'was not interested in developing the economy with a view to reducing unemployment or increasing the standard of living. He was a man of gestures, and this was one of them.'[21]

From an economic standpoint, Thermidor represents not so much a change of policy as a confirmation and consolidation of the policies which had been pursued, albeit somewhat contradictorily, by the Robespierrists since the beginning of 1794, a more positive shift in the direction of the original 1789–92 free-trade policies. Nevertheless, this shift was significant, and it was given greater impetus with the return of those Girondins who had escaped the guillotine, politicians who were even less convinced of the need for State intervention than the Robespierrists. During the winter of 1794–5, the most severe since 1709, the Thermidoreans gradually dismantled most, but not all, of the controls introduced in 1793, beginning in December with the abolition of the General Maximum. The winter is not the best time to liberalise prices, as the poor of Russia discovered recently. During the Directory, politicians, released from the tutelage of the sansculotterie who had been deprived of their armed force after the risings of the spring of 1795, would be more responsive to the needs of their new constituency – bankers, army contractors and generals. Hard currency would be

back by 1796, freedom of the grain trade on 9 June 1797; the following
year even saw the old municipal toll-gates being re-erected in Paris (27
vendémiaire Year VII/18 October 1798). They were a symbol, from the
standpoint of the urban poor whose suffering had increased demon-
strably after 1795, of a return, not to the early enthusiasms of 1789,
but to the hated excesses of the tax-farmers and customs officials of
the *ancien régime*.

Florin Aftalion believes that '. . . the return of a degree of economic
liberty allowed the French economy to recover slowly from the shock
of the Revolution'.[22] The shaky recovery after 1795 may be explained
by many other factors, including the creation of a French empire in
Europe, offering not only plunder in cash and kind, but new markets
for French goods, denied access to British and most colonial ports.
But what was the state of the French economy as the 1790s drew to its
bloody end? How had the Revolution affected French agriculture,
industry and overseas trade? So far as the last is concerned, the answer
is unequivocal – it had been a disaster. Between 1789 and 1799,
France's external trade probably halved in value, the trade with
America and the colonies being dealt an even more severe blow.[23]
Free-trade principles had never been applied in the French colonies;
they were, as was the case with the English, for home consumption
only. On 21 September 1793, the Convention had passed the Naviga-
tion Act, in the vain attempt to ensure that all goods were carried in
French ships. The problem was that there were fewer goods to carry,
the war with England, allied to upheavals in French colonies, having
ruined the lucrative re-export trade. This spelled, if not disaster, then
serious problems for the Atlantic and Mediterranean ports of
Marseille, Bordeaux and Nantes. Saint-Domingue, the 'jewel in the
crown' so far as France's colonial trade in the eighteenth century was
concerned, was lost as the first great black revolt in modern times, led
by Toussaint Louverture, destroyed the bases of the old planter
economy. Again, however, we need to note that France's trade with
her colonies, particularly in manufactured goods, had been declining
since the late 1770s.[24]

To get things really in perspective we need to look at the broader
canvas. Just as the politics of revolution cannot be understood
without reference to the 'Age of the Democratic Revolution', so
the economics of revolution must be placed in the wider context.
The Revolution redirected French trade and industry along lines
which followed the general switch of trade from a 'Mediterranean'
to an 'Atlantic' economy. One can detect a relationship here between
the decline – though certainly not the death – of the old 'proto-

industrial' textile products such as linen and wool, based mainly in the south and west, and the rise of the newer industries such as cotton, coal and iron, as well as the chemical industries which were based, again mainly, in the north and east of France. In order to present a balanced picture of the impact of the Revolution upon French trade and industry, we must return to this issue of long-term structures and place the developments of the 1790s within the longer time-sequence. The existence of traditional, 'proto-industrial' methods of production, which fitted snugly into a predominantly rural and seigneurial society, represents one of the most obvious but often neglected brakes upon the growth of modern French capitalism. France's economic growth in the eighteenth century, particularly in the textile industry, had occurred within the old proto-industrial economy, that is an economy run by family 'peasant-artisans', based upon small, often domestic, units of production, but producing for national and international markets. These older sectors of the economy were badly affected by the Revolution. Typical of the proto-industrial mentality was the case of the inhabitants of Longwy in the north-east of France who demanded in their *cahier de doléances* in 1789 that iron-masters should only be allowed to use wood after 'the local inhabitants had taken what they wanted'.[25] Or take the case of one of the most dynamic and gifted entrepreneurs in eighteenth-century France, Pierre-François Tubeuf. His attempt to concentrate and modernise the scores of small coal-mines in the Alès region of south-eastern France was defeated by the combined efforts of a *grand seigneur*, the marquis de Castries, and the bitter and violent resistance of hundreds of proto-industrial coal-miners, textile-workers, charcoal and lime-burners, eager to protect their independence and traditional way of life from the incursions of modern capitalism. Tubeuf, ruined by debt, eventually emigrated to America, there to die at the hands of local settlers, also vainly trying to protect a traditional socio-economic system.[26]

The Revolution undoubtedly aggravated the recession of the 1780s, reinforcing, in many ways, the proto-industrial mentality of peasants who divided their time between agricultural work in the spring and summer and making textiles in the late autumn and winter. The massive sale of National Lands meant that land, rather than trade or industry, became even more attractive as a source of investment. War, with its insatiable demand for men, food and animals, hyper-inflation and then the terrible winter of 1794 further disrupted the economy, so that by 1795-6 overall industrial production had reached its lowest point since 1789, possibly a drop of two-thirds.[27] Lyon, pride of the French silk industry, was seriously affected by the bloody civil war which had raged in its streets since 1793, helping to account for a 50 per cent drop in production.

But there were growth sectors, providing the nuclei of modern industrial capitalism. The cotton industry developed new techniques, particularly in the printed cotton sector: Fontaine-Guérard had invested 300,000 *livres* in his cotton ventures in the Eure department by 1792; Oberkampf had placed a similar sum in his Jouy-en-Josas works between 1790 and 1793. Imports of raw cotton rose from 4,800 tonnes in 1789 to 7,000 by 1803. At Rouen, 19,000 kilogrammes of printed cloth had been produced in 1789, 32,000 by 1800.[28] The metallurgical industry obviously benefited from the war. Cast-iron production more than doubled, from 50,000 *tonnes* to 120,000, between 1789 and 1800; although the number of blast furnaces fell from 600 to 500 in the same period, capacity increased indicating, as in the cotton sector, some technological innovation. On the other hand, coal production remained static at around 750,000 *tonnes*.

Revisionist historians, from Alfred Cobban to Emmanuel Le Roy Ladurie, have rightly insisted that, if one looks at the statistics of industrial or agricultural growth, or the substantial increase in the size of the small-scale farming sector, the French Revolution can in no way be described as a 'capitalist revolution'. They are surely right to insist that, certainly when compared with their great rival England, the period from 1789 to 1815 was, to put it at its best, a period of economic stagnation. *Marxisant* historians accept that there was little growth in the key industrial and agricultural sectors of the economy, although Albert Soboul, for example, would stress the fact that, in the cotton industry for one, there was significant technological and structural change. But their argument rests more upon the revolutionary consequences of the abolition of feudalism, the declining influence of the Catholic Church (opposed to usury), the abolition of the guilds, the introduction of anti-combination laws such as the Loi Chapelier of 1791, of the metric system, of a standardised system of weights and measures, of the shift from traditional, communitarian to modern contractual relationships between peasants and landlords, managers and workers. In other words, from a legal and juridical standpoint, France had taken a major, if not a giant, step on the road to a modern capitalist society. When evaluating the failure to match England's impressive spurt in those industries which were to be the sinews of a modern industrial society, such as coal and cotton, during the revolutionary and Napoleonic period, due attention has to be paid to the relatively massive peasant sector of France's economy before 1789 as well as to the extent of proto-industrial forms of manufacturing production. The sale of huge tracts of Church and *émigré* lands would undoubtedly retard the development of modern forms of industrialisation, if only by soaking up much-needed investment funds. This fact provides one of the major explanations for the slow pace of French industrialisation, when compared, as it invariably is, with the British model. Finally, one needs to ask how many investors would be inclined to put their money into risky industrial ventures during a period of war and instability which would last for over twenty years? The political economy of the revolutionary and Napoleonic period was, after all, a war economy. Grandiose notions of laissez-faire economics soon collapsed on the battlefields of Europe and the sea-lanes to the colonies, just as democratic politics had been placed on ice by the Jacobins during the Year II.

5 Social interpretations of the Revolution

It is now thirty years since Alfred Cobban, the 'father of revisionism', published his short book, *The Social Interpretation of the French Revolution*, provoking a fierce reaction from *marxisant* historians.[1] Cobban's attack was directed not so much against the importance of social and economic history as against the imposition of determinist, historical (that is marxist) laws of development. It is revealing that the socialist historian, Georges Lefebvre, came out relatively unscathed compared with the onslaught directed against the 'marxist–leninist' Albert Soboul. The attack upon Soboul reveals the implicit, often explicit, agenda of many revisionist historians – the rejection of the idea that *revolutionary* action advances the cause of 'progress', whether 'bourgeois' action during the English Civil War and the French Revolution, or 'peasant–proletarian' action during the Russian and Chinese revolutions of the present century. The collapse of the communist system in Europe over the past few years appears to have provided revisionists with historical justification for their anti-*marxisant* approach. Alfred Cobban rejected the notion that *revolution* was the essential midwife of the new bourgeois society in 1789, hence his emphasis upon the economic failure of the Revolution. In other words, revolutions actually impede, rather than advance, the capitalist process which, Professor Cobban agreed, had been developing in Europe over the previous three or four centuries. However, many present-day revisionist historians are, at best, only the illegitimate offspring of their father, placing far less emphasis than Cobban did on the importance of the social and the economic. For these historians, semiotics is more important than social history, *vieux-style*.

We argued in the previous chapter that, from a statistical and even a structural standpoint – the expansion of a small-owning peasant sector, for example – the French Revolution certainly did not produce a modern, urban, industrialised society. However, to deny the importance of the abolition of feudalism and the legal and juridical changes which the Revolution did introduce, all of which did mark an important stage in the evolution of French capitalism, is to barter historical truth for ideological advantage. This chapter will argue, taking a few selected areas of controversy between revisionist and *marxisant* historians, that, although it would be anachronistic to identify 'socialism' (the term was not employed widely until well into the nineteenth century) with the French Revolution, this does not invalidate the adoption of a *social* approach when evaluating the significance of certain key events. After all, if such an approach was good enough for Alfred Cobban . . .

When discussing the social history of the Revolution we should begin with the very important fact that there were far more French people around in 1789 than there had been a century earlier: approximately 21 million in 1700, 28 million by the 1790s. The rate of demographic growth slowed significantly during the last decades of the *ancien régime*, due, in part, to economic recession as well as to other factors such as the wider use of contraceptive techniques. Birth-rates fell from 38.8 per thousand during the 1780s to 32.9 per thousand by the early 1800s; death-rates also fell, from 35.5 per thousand in the period 1785–9 to 29.5 per thousand during the years 1795-9, the most striking feature being a big fall in infant mortality – 252 per thousand in the 1780s, 195 per thousand during the 1800s. These statistics alone suggest that a social 'revolution' was going on in homes throughout France – increased search for land to feed more mouths; changes in the structure of the family, especially the place of women in the home as well as in the workplace; attitudes to health and child-rearing. Finally, again on a human but rather more tragic note, it is worth recording that, despite the social upheavals of the Revolution and the half million deaths in wars, internal and external during the 1790s, the population of France would increase by twice this figure during the same period.[2]

Much of the strain which demographic change imposed upon French society fell upon country-dwellers. France, in 1789, was 85 per cent rural. Again, we noted in the previous chapter that much of the history of the Revolution can be reduced to a four-letter word – land. During the 1790s, 22 million French men and women lived in the countryside, 17-18 million of whom were engaged directly in what has been too hurriedly dismissed as 'agriculture'. Revisionist historians, anxious to improve the image of the *ancien régime* at the cost of the Revolution, too often ignore the social fact that the vast majority of these country-dwellers laboured within an increasingly despised and archaic feudal and theocratic system which exacted from those who worked the soil a multiplicity of dues and personal services. In 1789, the nobility, estimated to number between 300–400,000, owned, directly, around a fifth of the land of France, unequally dispersed with 40 per cent in parts of the south-west, 33 per cent in Burgundy, less than 10 per cent in Flanders. The Church, with approximately 170,000 clerics, possessed under one-tenth of the land, although its landed influence varied from 5 per cent in parts of the west to 20 per cent in parts of the north and east, another very significant socio-economic fact. It is now widely accepted, even by many revisionist historians that there was a 'seigneurial reaction' during the second half of the eighteenth century, associated, as Professor Cobban himself suggested, with the incursion of capitalist values into the management of estates. The seizure of common lands, the attack on customary rights, the use of lawyers and agents to scrutinise title-deeds so that more could be squeezed from the peasantry, already suffering from increasing State taxation as well as from the payment of the Church tithe, all transformed an unacceptable system into an intolerable one for those who worked the land. Annie Moulin has suggested that if one adds up the seigneurial taxes and dues which the French peasant paid to his lord, the tithe (*dîme*) levied by his local church, and the taxes, direct and indirect, which went to the government, we are looking at a loss to the peasant 'of between one-quarter and one-half of the revenue of the peasant household'.[3]

The *Grande Peur*, that massive, six-pronged assault which swept through France during the spring and summer of 1789, launched within the context of the political events in Paris, performed the last rites over a defunct feudal system. On 4 August, the deputies declared that 'feudalism was abolished in its entirety'. In other words, the social struggle of the peasantry against an anachronistic system of feudal expropriation precipitated the most momentous event of the Revolution – the root and branch attack upon the social, political and institutional structure of *ancien régime* France. This is not a conclusion drawn by *marxisant* historians alone: William Doyle, for example, gives it the right emphasis:

But far more than feudalism had been cast aside on the night of 4 August. Privilege, that fundamental principle of social and institutional life since time immemorial, had been renounced. . . . For three centuries French social mobility had largely been channelled through the sale of offices, but that too now stood condemned.[4]

One wonders how any historian can sustain the argument that the Revolution was, *au fond*, a political event with social consequences! At the heart of the Revolution lay the social conflict which, for more than a century, had pitted peasant against the seigneurial system. After 4 August, it became a matter of squabbling over the rich spoils. Here again, the peasants were not to go away empty-handed. No wonder that, towards the end of his distinguished career, Albert Soboul preferred to talk of the French Revolution not as a 'capitalist, bourgeois' revolution but as a 'peasant-bourgeois' revolution.[5]

However, it would take another three years, at least, to begin to clear the débris of feudalism. This was primarily due to the continued existence of the nobility which had lost its pre-eminence, but certainly not all its power and influence over the land, as well as the existence of profound divisions within peasant society itself. There was also the crucial political fact of the break-up of the peasant–bourgeois alliance which alone had secured the victory over the common enemy – feudalism – in 1789. Far from ending conflict in the countryside, the introduction of a new agrarian system based upon property contracts, together with the sale and redistribution of around 10 per cent of the land of France, mainly 'nationalised' Church property, was bound to increase antagonisms between peasants seeking more land and the wealthy bourgeoisie, urban and rural, as well as aggravating, and *politicising*, long-standing, festering conflicts between rich and poor peasants themselves. There was, after all, not that much in common between the wealthy farmers, the *laboureurs* and *gros fermiers* at the top, who had often acted as agents of the absentee noble and cleric, leasing from them the right to collect feudal and clerical dues, the small-owning peasants (*petits propriétaires*) in the middle, and the millions of share-croppers (*métayers*) – working perhaps as many as two-thirds of all French farms – and day-labourers (*journaliers*) who formed over half of the community in the richer cereal-growing regions of the north or around Paris.

Applying the *coup de grâce* to a feudal regime, already mortally wounded by the socio-economic and intellectual onslaughts launched in the decades preceding the Revolution, was relatively easy, particularly given the wide social consensus which provided the heavy ammunition, although, it needs to be repeated, the actual *coup de grâce* was the work of the peasants themselves during the *Grande Peur*. However, the collapse of this consensus, central to an understanding of the subsequent course of the Revolution, was the problem. The first real signs of the break-up of the *bourgeois–peasant* alliance of the summer of 1789 came with the legislation of the spring of 1790 which attempted to resolve the thorny problems associated with the collapse of the feudal system of land tenure. For example, thousands of non-nobles had bought seigneuries before 1789, their contracts including the right to levy landed and other, even 'feudal' dues, from their tenants and share-croppers. Were they now to be deprived of all this income? What about the 'rights of property', lynch-pin of the new, modern, contractual order? What of the *dîme*, a due which had often been incorporated into landed contracts? Would the landowner carry the cost of abolition? The seemingly obsessive bourgeois concern with 'the rights of property' during the 1790s, increasingly regarded as more sacred than the Catholic mass, cannot be understood without placing it in the context of the abolition of feudal property relations and the seizure of Church lands. The most modern aspect of the French Revolution was the time and energy it devoted to securing 'property-rights', still a fundamental issue in contemporary European society.

The National Assembly, after lengthy discussions in its Feudal Committee, decided that, apart from the Church *dîme* and the dues associated with personal servitude, which were to be abolished without compensation (in theory again), all 'landed' dues would have to be redeemed at 20 or 25 times their annual value. Peasants would have to prove, by producing the original title-deed, that a particular due was 'landed' rather than 'feudal'. But this was an almost impossible task given the complexity of feudal documents, to say nothing of their disappearance during the *Grande Peur*. Peasants felt cheated. The land was theirs. Why should they pay anything, other than a fair rent to their landlords? The conflict over the transformation of feudal into bourgeois, individual property rights produced the first major crack between what Patrice Higonnet has called 'bourgeois universalism', and the apparently confused, but historically explicable, peasant ideal of ownership within a traditional, communitarian socio-economic framework. Hence, the refusal on the part of the vast majority of peasants to redeem what they regarded as illegal dues; hence, the periodic waves of peasant insurrection which afflicted the French countryside until 1793.

Once again, war, as well as the political situation in Paris, helped to resolve the problem in favour of the peasantry. It is no coincidence that the two legislative acts passed in August 1792 and June of the following year, actually abolishing the 'feudal regime', came at a time when the war was going badly and the monarchy was being overthrown. To survive, the Girondins needed the mass support of the peasantry and that support was draining away. Feudalism had to go, *de facto* as well as *de jure*. If one compares the victory of the French peasantry with that of their Russian counterparts who, following the Emancipation of Serfdom Act of 1861, were forced to go on paying redemption dues for *forty years*, one has some idea of the magnitude of the victory secured in just four years by the French peasantry. Most historians agree that the scale of this victory, by strengthening the existence of a massive peasant sector of French society, largely determined the future character of French society.

But was modern capitalism in France strengthened by this victory? What of the idea (more leninist than marxist!) that hundreds of thousands of 'democratic' small-owning peasants could accumulate enough capital to assist in the launch, eventually, of the real bourgeois industrial revolution? François Hincker argues that 'the fantastic drop in obligatory payments opened up immense perspectives'.[6] There is no doubt that peasants did acquire property from the massive sale of Church lands. Although the bourgeoisie, urban and rural, got the lion's share – selling by auction made it easier for the wealthy to triumph – tens of thousands of peasants joined in the biggest land-rush in French history. Georges Lefebvre has estimated that, in the department of the Nord, a staggering 25 per cent of the land was sold as *biens nationaux*, with the peasantry and the bourgeoisie sharing the spoils between them, though this was the exception rather than the rule.[7] However, let us note that, in the Chartres region, for example, the number of landowners did increase by 30 per cent between 1790 and 1820 'but the peasant majority ended up with most of the holdings of less than 5 *hectares*'.[8] In the final analysis, *marxisant* theses concerning the link between the advance of modern capitalism and the existence of a large small-owning peasant society do not entirely convince. If the number of small peasant owners increased substantially, often through resales, the methods of farming the land underwent very little change. In other words, for the most part, peasants, large and small, got land but proceeded to farm it in the traditional way, leasing out a few acres to share-croppers, refusing to carve up the common lands, persisting with traditional rights of gleaning and pasturing. In addition, many of the more marginal farmers and share-croppers, holding none of the right cards for this particular poker game, lost out altogether. For them, the rapacious *laboureur* or tenant-farmer replaced the old *seigneur* as the new hate-figure. One small farmer from the commune of Seyne (Gard) put it succinctly: the Revolution had benefited France by ridding the country of nobles and priests: 'it only remains for us to strike down the big landowners (*gros propriétaires fonciers*), because it is now that they are beginning to use their clout to oppress the poor inhabitants of the countryside'.[9] The French road to capitalism would include many detours where more communitarian, 'socialist' ideals, many of then inherited from France's peasant past, continued to thrive.

One hotly debated issue concerns the response of the Jacobins to the social crisis which the Revolution had unleashed in the countryside. Did they have a coherent social policy? It would be absurd to expect it to be too coherent given the quite exceptional military and political circumstances of the Year II. However, there is recent research which suggests that the Jacobin Terror was not just a product of war, or of the totalitarian day-dreams of Maximilien Robespierre; its ideology was also shaped by the social and economic consequences of the abolition of the *ancien régime*. This is not to argue that the Jacobins were 'proto-socialists', certainly not in the marxist sense of a revolutionary vanguard that believed in the necessity of class struggle and the expropriation of bourgeois property – far from it. However, one historian has argued recently that there may well be a link between the Jacobins and early French socialists, such as Fourier and Saint-Simon, who also rejected the necessity of violent revolution, the class struggle and the abolition of private property.[10] This would fit with the conclusions of Peter Jones's recent research concerning the creation of a property-owning democracy during the Year II.

Let us take the plans to redistribute *émigré* property to the poor and the even more contentious issue of common lands, an issue which had lined up communities against *seigneurs* ever since the latter had been given the right to seize one-third of the commons in 1669. Legislation on these crucial matters was passed from 3-10 June 1793, and the reactions highlight the complexity of the struggle between rich and poor, agrarian individualists and collectivists. In some regions, rich farmers owning cattle or sheep, anxious to continue their monopoly of the use of common lands, did not want to see them divided up amongst the poor; on the other hand, if they wanted more land to plough and were interested in enclosures then clearly division might be attractive. In June 1793, the Jacobins attempted to resolve the issue in favour of the small farmer. By the legislation of 10 June, communities could divide the commons amongst the heads of households, given that one-third of the community voted in favour. Jones shows that poorer peasants did benefit from the division of the common lands in some regions, whilst further legislation permitting the sale of *émigré* lands was implemented in favour of the poor. However, the experiment was short-lived; the Thermidoreans gradually whittled away the minor gains of the Year II. As Jones concludes, Jacobin policy was 'flawed and they failed'.[11] None the less, the Jacobins did have a *social* (though not socialist) policy.

The overall point to make is that one does not have to sleep with *Das Capital* under one's pillow to recognise the relationship between socio-economic developments and the political evolution of the French Revolution, just as one does not have to swallow (even if one puts some Gramscian sugar on the marxist pill) too direct a relationship between the 'superstructure' – cultural, legal and juridical – and the socio-economic 'base'. Geoffrey Ellis, an informed critic of *marxisant* theories, can write, *à propos* the sale of *biens nationaux*, 'By any standards, the sale of such vast resources was a major social and economic development in France during the 1790s.'[12] The Revolution did effect a major redistribution of land. In 1789, the Church had owned up to 10 per cent of the land of France, the nobility twice as much; by 1815, the Church had ceased to be a major landowner whilst the nobility had lost perhaps half of its property. However, it is equally important to make the point that the two most important social events of the Revolution – the collapse of the feudal system and the sale of 10 per cent of the land of France – did not produce an agrarian revolution on the English model. Certainly, under the Directory, we can discern a more individualist and 'free-market' approach to agriculture, but Arthur Young's dreams of a happy French community of farmers, retired from the commons behind their enclosures, would only be realised in part.

One area of social history which requires further research concerns the symbiotic relationship between agriculture and industry in the French countryside. One has become accustomed to use the term 'peasant' without thinking what it actually encompasses. Hundreds of thousands of French 'peasants' spent half the year in the fields, their own and other people's, the other half spinning and weaving for France's massive textile industry which had expanded at a dramatic rate in certain regions of France – around Lille in the north-east, Rouen in the west, Nîmes in the south-east, for example – particularly after the edicts of the 1760s which allowed peasants to work without being members of a guild. The village of Roubaix near the commercial and manufacturing centre of Lille, for example, had increased its population from 4,500 in the 1760s to 12,000 by 1789. In the twenty parishes around the city of Rennes in the west, one in four of the total population of 26,000 was engaged in the production of sail-cloth:

'That is, rural industry contributed to the livelihood of virtually every family in the region.'[13] Nîmes, in the south-east of France, was the centre of a textile industry which linked scores of villages and *bourgs* within a radius of twenty miles or more. Far too little is known about the impact of the Revolution upon these workers, particularly upon female workers. As war, inflation and recession impacted upon the countryside, many village communities, their numbers swollen by men who had been employed in the towns when work was available, fell back upon their own resources, making their own clothes, tools and utensils. In the Lower Languedoc region, many villages began to plant hemp again in order to produce rough cloth for clothes and sacks. Given the scale of the economic recession in France from the 1780s to the 1800s, their lot was not a happy one, but we need to know far more about all this.

How did proto-industrial workers respond to the Revolution? The answer is that no general pattern is discernible. One way of unlocking the mystery is to consider first the socio-cultural nature of the community, and second their relationship to those who provided them with their livelihoods. The indications are, depending on these and other factors, that proto-industrial workers, caught between the rural and the urban world, could opt for or against the Revolution. Let us take the example of the departments of the Ardèche and the Gard in Lower Languedoc, whose communities had been increasingly drawn into the textile – particularly woollens and silks – industry in the eighteenth century. There is evidence of continuity in the poor, mainly Catholic region of the Bas-Vivarais between the insurrections of the 1780s – the *masques armés* revolt of 1783, for example – and the Catholic royalist movements of the 1790s, the *camps de Jalès* and the actions of the *égorgeurs* during the Directory. In the mainly Protestant villages of the Gardonnenque, north-east of Nîmes, on the other hand, there was a close religious and economic dependency upon the rich Protestant *négociants* of the city. In the summer of 1790, when the first elections of the Revolution were taking place in Nîmes, thousands of Protestant proto-industrial workers poured down from the hills to support the Protestant ticket, participating in the massacre of hundreds of Catholic workers, the first major, bloody manifestation of counter-revolution in France. The link between social distress and political action is evident, but the importance of religious affiliation obviously helps to explain revolutionary or counter-revolutionary options.[14]

Donald Sutherland and Tim LeGoff open up the possibility of links between social distress, counter-revolution and crime in the Haute-

Loire region which witnessed the near total collapse of lace-making during the 1790s: 'Since the export of these textiles paid for the grain which the region had to import because it was not cereal country, everyone suffered and the surrounding region became notorious for its draft-dodging, banditry and general crime.'[15] As disenchantment with the Revolution increased, links between draft-dodging, crime and 'counter-revolution' were reinforced. There is also a relationship between Charles Tilly's thesis concerning rapid and uneven rates of urbanisation and the spread of proto-industrialisation in the countryside which has not yet been fully explored. Again, the key question so far as the counter-revolution in the Vendée is concerned is why did some artisan communities choose the republican option whilst others rejected it? Religious differences are not the answer here, but there is the common thread, between counter-revolutionary movements in the west and those in the south-east, concerning the degree of economic dependence which existed between the urban merchants, who provided the work and the markets, and their work-force. The leader of the counter-revolution in Nîmes in 1790, François Froment, accused local merchant-manufacturers of giving work only to Protestant rural villagers who were prepared to do it more cheaply. For the Vendée, Paul Bois offers a more sociological approach suggesting that, in order to explain the choice of political options, we should distinguish between 'weavers grouped in bourgs, producing for foreign markets, and more dependent upon urban influences, and those who, working for local needs, were immersed in a peasant world, the true criterion of *mentalité* being less what profession they exercised than the social environment'.[16] This approach, presumably, would win the approval of the younger generation of 'socio-cultural' historians.

For example, David Garrioch and Michael Sonenscher have reopened the debate on urban artisans, suggesting more sophisticated ways of understanding historical change and political choice during the revolutionary period. In his original work on the patterns and processes of eighteenth-century urban trades, Michael Sonenscher has been at pains to 'deconstruct' the relationship between a worker's place in the production process and the politics of the Year II as posited by Albert Soboul in his classic *Les Sansculottes parisiens de l'An II* (Paris, 1959). Soboul argued that the small artisan and shopkeeper stratum of Paris society, pressurised by the rise of modern forms of capitalism, developed a political programme, related certainly to the peculiar circumstances of the Year II, but also to the experience of declining artisans and urban consumers for whom the main enemy was commercial capitalism. Sonenscher, however, rejects what he (in common with Alfred Cobban) considers to be too ideologically rigid a link between political choice and the world of work: 'artisans who became sansculottes did not always do so because they were artisans'. In a joint article, Garrioch and Sonenscher noted, for example, that the *compagnonnage* organisation for journeymen was not prevalent in Paris, and that 'There were other types of association, which, while conforming to the general pattern of eighteenth-century French sociability, drew upon the particularities of local environment.'[17]

Kinship, the complex and shifting patterns of work associated with sub-contracting, and the development of a 'language of labour' developed in the struggle against the evolution of merchant capitalism and articulated through the pre-revolutionary courts, these are issues which are attracting attention: they appear to be confirmed by the memoirs of one Parisian artisan, Jacques Ménétra.[18] The adoption of a more sociological approach is to be welcomed as is the subtlety of argument and the weight of erudition, but it is surely throwing the social baby out with the marxist bathwater to conclude that 'the social determinants of the politics of the Year II simply did not exist'.[19] There *was* an artisan 'ideology', derived, no doubt, from a wider range of socio-cultural experience than that allowed for by Albert Soboul, and which certainly did not spring fully armed from the work-bench or the politics of the Year II, but which none the less sought to defend a democracy of small-scale producers from developing forms (plural not singular) of modern capitalism. Gwyn Williams, in an essay called 'Twenty years after' to introduce a new edition of his *Artisans and Sansculottes* remarks: 'The original conclusion of my book bears repeating. The ideology of democracy was pre-industrial and its first serious practitioners were artisans.'[20] Recalling Peter Jones's argument in favour of the existence of a Jacobin 'social policy', I would further argue that the Jacobin–sansculotte alliance of 1793 was not based solely on the pragmatic political and military realities of the period, but on an admittedly loose – and even fanciful perhaps – shared perception of a society which could recognise both individualism, property-rights *and* community. In this, the Jacobins shared the ideological 'universalism' of the bourgeoisie of 1789. Echoes of the fusion of 'individualism' and community can even be heard today.

We have dealt with the social question so far as viewed 'from below'. What was happening 'from above'? What was the impact of the Revolution upon the industrialists, manufacturers and merchants who had served their apprenticeship during the *ancien régime*? Here the contrast between *marxisant* and revisionist historians is more stark. Albert Soboul stressed the development of modern forms of industrial capitalism, the cotton, coal and iron-ore industries, the entrepreneurial dynamism of ironmasters such as Dietrich who employed 800 workers at his Niederbronn works alone; or the de Wendel family with their forges at Charleville, Homburg and Hayange; or the Anzin coal-mining company, one of the biggest in Europe, employing 4,000 men. Typically, Soboul concludes: 'The sight of this economic activity made the men of the bourgeoisie conscious of their class and made them understand that their interests were irreparably opposed to those of the aristocracy.'[21] From the revisionist camp, Guy Chaussinand-Nogaret absolutely refutes the idea that there was a relationship between development of industrial capitalism and the 'rise of the bourgeoisie'. For the latter, as we have seen, it was the aristocracy, not the bourgeoisie who was in the vanguard of a modern capitalist revolution:

> Over a whole range of activities and enterprises nobles, either alone or in association with members of the greater business bourgeoisie, showed their dynamism, their taste for invention and innovation, and their ability as economic leaders: by which I mean their ability to direct capital originating in land or government stock into productive activities . . . to transmute the forms of production into an industrial revolution.[22]

Again, the argument, taken at face-value, is persuasive. Take coal-mining: the prince de Croy was a leading figure behind the Anzin coal-mining company; half of the iron-forges in France were owned by nobles, like the de Wendels and the Dietrichs.

Again, however, there are serious flaws in the argument. To leave aside for the moment the prevailing anti-industrial and commercial ethos of *ancien régime* France, many of the 'nobles' cited had been recently ennobled (Dietrich as late as 1761) and were far from being typical of their order. In addition, it has to remembered that the nobility owned most of the land beneath which the coal, iron-ore, and other mineral deposits lay; their involvement was often regarded as just another way of increasing revenues from their landed estates. Only a minority of nobles managed industrial concerns directly; more often than not they were 'farmed-out' to entrepreneurs who were forced to work within the constraints of a seigneurial, proto-industrial society. My recent study of the epic struggle between the 'bourgeois', Pierre-François Tubeuf, and the 'aristocrat', maréchal de Castries, for control of the coal-mining region of the Basses-Cévennes, reveals the essential difference in 'economic behaviour'. Whilst the mining expert Tubeuf invested massive sums in his mines, concentrated production in a few key places, introduced new techniques for mining coal, the maréchal de Castries, possessing seigneurial control over the land beneath which the most productive mines were to be found, worked through his agents and stewards who were constantly urging him not to involve himself too deeply in modern industrial ventures (*les entreprises en grand*). Ownership, in terms of land or shares, is not the key issue here; it is more a question of *how*, in terms of investment, technical innovation, concentration, and 'man-management', industrial concerns were worked.

What is also interesting, however, is the fact that one of France's leading entrepreneurs, Tubeuf, did not actually emigrate until 1791, suggesting that the Revolution did not exactly create a capitalist nirvana, at least for those involved in heavy industry. Two pieces of legislation passed in that year underline the degree to which the revolutionary child did not emancipate itself fully from the *ancien régime* man: the Rural Code of 27 September, although moving in the direction of agrarian individualism, left considerable scope for the maintenance of traditional farming customs; the legislation on mining (12–28 July 1791) was a blow for those who, like Tubeuf, wanted the State to support the granting of large mining concessions, article three making it abundantly plain that the small landowner, scratching a fox-hole into the hillside to get coal, would be given preference. Again, one should not attempt to understand why this legislation was passed in the form it was without placing it in the context of *increasing* social discontent from small peasant landowners, as well as from the dispossessed. It could be argued that the situation was far worse for financiers and merchants: this was still, after all, a world dominated by commercial, not industrial, capitalism. Indeed, bankers, tax-farmers, and the merchant class – wholesalers rather than retailers – paid a high price during the Terror. Over 30 tax-farmers were executed. In Lyon, almost one-quarter of the 1,900 official executions were drawn from the commercial sector; in Nîmes, out of the 133 executions, there were 4 *négociants*, 5 manufacturers and 13 merchants.

However, we have argued earlier that it was the outbreak of war, more than the outbreak of the Revolution, which caused major problems for merchants, externally with the loss of France's rich colonies, internally, with the onset of the Terror. The Atlantic ports of the west were not seriously affected until 1793, Bordeaux a little earlier. The international summer fair at Beaucaire on the Rhône was still attracting a healthy attendance in the early 1790s. The success of these major ports continued to stimulate the manufactures and commerce of neighbouring inland regions, in the case of Nantes and Le Havre, all the way to Paris where by the late 1790s, 40,000 workers would be engaged in producing the multifarious 'articles de Paris'. During the early stages of the Revolution, the strength of the commercial and trading sector was mirrored on the political stage. Lynn Hunt has shown how this sector, although not well represented at the national level – from 14 per cent of the National Assembly in 1790 to 4 per cent under the Directory – played a central role in most important cities and towns until 1793: half the posts on the Marseille council were filled by merchants during the early years of the Revolution; they occupied two-thirds of the 'federalist' council in Bordeaux elected in early 1793.

The debate on the Federalist Revolt of the summer of 1793 is again an area where some historians have striven hard to deny the link between socio-economic and political forces. Recently, Antonio De Francesco has challenged 'the seeping social characterization of the Federalist revolt'. In place of a social interpretation, the author prefers to concentrate on political and institutional issues, the election of new men at local level after 1792 dedicated to democratic politics, the importance of local institutions, in general terms 'the breakdown of the political relationship between the capital and the provinces'.[23] Many of these points have, in fact, been integrated into the interpretations provided by two detailed studies of federalism, the first by Paul Hanson, comparing 'federalist' Caen with 'Montagnard' Limoges, the second by Bill Edmonds focusing upon the major insurrection in Lyon. However, although there are distinct differences of emphasis concerning the explanation of the relationship between the merchant/ manufacturing elites and the popular masses (the social composition of federalist cities were, after all, different), both agree that socio-economic factors are central to an analysis of provincial politics. Hanson concludes that 'the social fabric and economic structures of a town and region are crucial factors in molding the shape of the local political arena';[24] whilst Edmonds, although emphasising the political significance of the ham-fisted nature of Jacobin policy towards Lyon, pursues a similar line when he writes that 'deep social divisions prevented Lyon from showing a united front to outsiders or taking the line of *attentisme*: timely adjustment to changes of direction in Paris'.[25] I would take precisely the same line with respect to the federalist revolt in Nîmes. The notion that the wealthy *négociants* and merchant/ manufacturers of the big commercial cities had the best interests of their work-forces at heart flies in the face of all the evidence concerning their appalling attitude towards workers in the pre-revolutionary period. De Francesco is on safer ground when he argues, albeit with some exaggeration, that the Jacobins 'in the name of popular rule and by means of a tax on wealth and the call for a generalized *maximum*, destroyed the economic balance of the most advanced areas of France, and carried out their policies with authoritarian ruthlessness'.[26] But then this was a period of 'total war'.

The Directorial regime between 1795 and 1799 cannot be understood without an appreciation of the damage which the Terror had inflicted upon the economic elites: for one of the Directors, Barras, as for Napoleon, it was impossible to conduct total war without the support of war contractors and bankers. The Directory would signal a marked shift in the direction of the Revolution, away from the public to the private. Howard Brown, in his study of the relationship between the Directory and war contractors, has referred to the 'drive to privatize'. Certainly those involved in the financial, manufacturing and commercial sectors could not only breathe again after the constraints of the Terror, but set about restoring, or creating *ab initio*, personal fortunes. Brown even suggests that the Directory's method of prosecuting war, fraught with social consequences for the ordinary people of France, was the eighteenth-century equivalent of 'the twentieth-century military/industrial complex'.[27] From 1795 to 1799, the gap between *les gros* and *les petits* widened dangerously, a clue to the continuity of counter-revolutionary, or should we say, 'anti-revolutionary' activity. Again, far more research needs to be conducted on the relationship between the political and economic policies of the Directory and the recrudescence of widespread social unrest, often taking the form of 'counter-revolution'.

Despite the obvious discontinuities, there were, of course, patterns of continuity during the 1790s. Not everyone, for example, who had been involved in trade and manufacturing in 1789 had been killed off by the late 1790s. Many colonies had been lost it is true (although trade with them did not necessarily cease), but the increasing exclusion of British goods was creating new markets internally and externally. There was also the possibility of acquiring new sites from the sale of national lands. Between 1790 and 1802, cotton manufacturers alone acquired eighty-two such properties. Cotton was one of the success stories of the Revolution and the history of Cristophe Oberkampf proves that the Revolution could promote modern industrial techniques. Producing 37,000 pieces of printed cotton cloth in 1791, this figure had risen to 58,000 by 1809. One should remember that Oberkampf had been a good revolutionary, mayor of his commune situated near Paris, a member of its Popular Society. None the less, there can be no possible doubt that things were far easier after 1795.

Another industrialist on a European scale was Guillaume Ternaux, one of those who had decided, during the Terror, that emigration was the better part of survival. But he was back by 1798 to create one of the biggest textile and furnishing concerns in France, employing, by the 1820s, 19,000 workers. Paul Butel stresses that the Revolution promoted a much bigger national market with a 'spectacular rise' in the number of new industries in Paris and to the east: 'The Directory was a time of prosperity, and from 1796 onwards machine spinning increased substantially following the modernisation of the cotton mills.'[28]

Finally, when considering the social history of the financial and manufacturing elites, we should point to those studies which confirm the continuity, rather than the ruptures in the economic history of the Revolution. Bordeaux had around the same number of merchants in 1799 as it had had in 1789; Gail Bossenga tells us that, by 1810, 60 per cent of the Lille municipal council was drawn from the merchant and manufacturing class.[29] In Paris, bankers, currency dealers, war contractors and *négociants* dominated the list of the 150 highest taxpayers in the capital in 1808.[30] Apart from highlighting the vast fortunes made by bankers such as Jean-Frédéric Perregaux – treasurer to the Committee of Public Safety and the Napoleonic Consulate – Michel Brugière's study of the financial and manufacturing elite during the Revolution also stresses the continuity of personnel from 1789 to the Empire. Men like F. Rolland, son of a rich textile family from Carcassonne who opened a spinning-mill near Paris in 1801; Lecouteulx de Canteleu, banker, arrested during the Terror, but who survived to become the first president of the Bank of France; or F-P. Cornut de la Fontaine, secretary to the royal Treasury in 1789, chief cashier of the Bank of France from 1803–8.[31] It was easier for the rich and the influential to devise strategies for survival than it was for the sansculottes, whose enemies they had been during the Year II.

Survival, even in physical terms, was far harder for the poor. In his *Tableau de Paris* Louis-Sébastien Mercier writes that one-quarter of the population of the capital 'does not know from one day to the next whether its labours will bring in enough to live on on the morrow'.[32] The Revolution did little to allay their fears, although, as with the 'abolition of feudalism' announced in 1789, we are confronted with an even wider gap between revolutionary idealism and harsh reality. It could be argued that no regime in modern history *thought* of doing more for the poor. During the Constituent Assembly, the *Comité de mendicité*, under its humanitarian president, La Rochefoucauld-

Liancourt, undertook a most exhaustive survey of poverty, its causes and cures. The results of its inquiries were disturbing, to say the least: 'For in fifty-one departments . . . the Committee estimated that the number of *mendiants* was an astonishing 1,928,064 out of a total population of 16,634,466, or almost one in eight of the total.'[33] Before a coherent welfare policy could be implemented, the government had to fall back upon the *ancien régime* palliative of *ateliers de charité*. During the Terror, the State actually began to compile a record of all those in need of welfare (the *Grand Livre de Bienfaisance*), and began doling out money to orphans and widows. The ideal surpassed, or at least equalled, the aspirations of politicians in the 1940s to create welfare provision 'from the cradle to the grave'. But war and lack of funds gnawed away at such laudable ambitions. There were also the contradictions inherent in so much of the social legislation of the Revolution. The abolition of feudalism, municipal taxes, the seizure of hospital property, as well as the eventual attack on the Catholic Sisters of Charity, meant that, by 1796, hospitals were in a parlous condition, worse off, in the vast majority of cases, than they had been in 1789. Once again, as with education, the infant secular State had bitten off more than it could chew.

Perhaps more than it wanted to chew, particularly after the Terror when fear of the poor haunted the dreams of all property-owners. The Thermidoreans and their successors seized upon the failure of early revolutionary policy to switch welfare provision back to the 'private sector'. *Ateliers de charité* were closed, leaving the really poor 'destitute and bewildered'; the duty of caring for the poor was thrust back upon the municipalities, reliant more upon private charity than State provision. As a result, the last years of the 1790s proved a nightmare for the really poor. Many preferred to risk life and limb on the battlefields abroad than fight for survival at home: the battlefields of Europe represented the real 'outdoor relief' for the more miserable sections of the population. Richard Cobb has charted the dismal fate of hundreds of men and women, mostly the former, who were driven to suicide in Paris between 1795 and 1801. The author is adept at evoking sympathy for these pathetic social victims fished out of the Seine, whose gaudy apparel – the 'harlequined' poor – masked the drab misery of their existence. One victim, in particular, may be taken to symbolise the fate of the many. On one of the copper buttons of his coat was stamped the ironic legend 'République française'.[34] Florin Aftalion is convinced that the 'free-market' policies of the Thermidoreans were not to blame for the mass misery of post-1795 France, but Alan Forrest is surely nearer the mark when he concludes that 'the poor could be excused for thinking by the end of the decade that the Revolution they had lived through was not their revolution at all but one devoted to the interests of others, of the bourgeois, of the towns, of Paris, of people who had little knowledge or understanding of their plight'.[35]

If in class terms the poor suffered most during the Revolution, in terms of gender it could be argued that the female of the species suffered more than the male. Marxist historians of the previous generation, consumed with class and structure, paid less heed than they might have done to women. One of the most original of his kind, Gwyn Williams, in an introduction to a new edition of his *Artisans and Sansculottes*, first published in 1968, begs forgiveness, with some Celtic overkill: 'Twenty years on, however, I cannot fail to note, in pain and shame, the barely concealed *surprise* [at women's participation in the Revolution] which informs my writing at that point.[36] Some of my own students are still surprised to learn that the Revolution produced a *Declaration of the Rights of Woman* as well as the more famous *Rights of Man*. However, the tide is turning, although, despite the pioneering work of female historians as different and as gifted as Olwen Hufton and Darlene Levy, it is still certainly not at the flood. Due and proper emphasis is now being placed on the crucial importance of the March to Versailles on 5 October 1789 when *women* captured the monarchy for Paris and the Revolution for ordinary people, much more frightening for the bourgeois elites in the Constituent Assembly than the attack on the Bastille; on the contribution of women to the genesis and objectives of revolutionary – not just food – riots; on their contribution to the creation of women's political consciousness through clubs like the *Société des Républicaines-Révolutionnaires*; and, finally, on women's resistance to the religious changes wrought by the Revolution and to the revival of Catholicism in France after 1795.[37] On the critical period of the Terror, however, far more needs to be done on the relationship between the women's movement, the *Enragés* and the response of Girondins and Jacobins during those crucial months of March–June 1793, as well as on the political role of women after Thermidor, something which Babeuf, like some of the *Enragés* sought to encourage. There can be absolutely no doubt that, by 1795, men had become thoroughly frightened concerning the potential for a women's revolution within the Revolution. After 1795, women were not even admitted, unaccompanied, into the spectators' gallery of its national assemblies.

It is all the more important to stress the importance of the political contribution of women in shaping the course and character of the

Revolution, since all too often serious consideration of this aspect of their history is omitted. None the less, the vast majority of Frenchmen continued to regard women as the gentler sex, peculiarly fashioned for bringing life into the world and caring for it once arrived. And this women continued to do on a scale, given the vicissitudes of the Revolution, which was little short of heroic. Modern history is characterised by another division of labour than the economic concept produced by Adam Smith – a gender division which sees men doing the killing and women clearing up the human mess. (Did David have this thought in mind when he painted his *Les Sabines* in 1799?). Throughout the Revolution, officially or unofficially, it was women in the religious nursing orders who cared for the sick and the dying; it was women who kept families together when the men joined the vast armies of the 1790s; women and children died alongside their partners and fathers in the Vendéean wars; women who continued to run the small units of production, in home, workshop or business when their husbands died, again, a neglected area of research. In Lille, for example, 'widow Bernard Mousson' managed the operation of twenty spinning-mills producing linen thread.[38] From the Enlightenment to the late nineteenth century, a woman who dedicated herself to a political career or cause continued to have her sex called into question.[39] But even if the revolutionary Pantheon was to be reserved strictly for men, this, in itself, opens up new ways of thinking about the nature of the 'bourgeois Revolution', as Hazel Mills has suggested recently, in an informative survey of the entire subject. The impact of 'feminism' upon the historiography of the Revolution is beginning to open up new avenues of research, something which was happening in the *Cercle Social* and among the *Enragés* during the early 1790s.[40]

6 Revolutionary culture: the creation of *'l'homme nouveau'*

One of the most obvious indications that the marxist paradigm has been under severe attack over the past decade is the fact that 'culture' has replaced 'class' as a focus of scholarly concern. Emmet Kennedy's recent comprehensive textbook, *The Culture of the French Revolution*, opens with the statement: 'The French Revolution was a profound cultural event.'[1] It was. Too often in the past, the cultural history of the Revolution has been relegated to a brief résumé of the individual contributions of 'great names' – David, Houdon, Chénier, Grétry, Gossec taking pride of place. The most important service rendered by revisionist historians has been the emphasis they have placed upon 'political culture', although some have undoubtedly exaggerated its significance, particularly its autonomy in relation to the social and the economic.

Many scholars, whose intellectual formation has often been shaped by the disciplines of linguistics, sociology, ethnography and anthropology, have provided us with a broader framework within which to evaluate the cultural experience of those who lived through the 1790s. Language, for example, has been 'deconstructed', then reconstructed to possess almost nuclear power. For Sandy Petrey, 'The French Revolution was explosively consistent in its determination to do things with words', the word *aristocrate* possessing 'staggering political force'.[2] Eric Walter has reconstructed Gracchus Babeuf, who 'secularises the figure of Jesus to the point of denying his divinity . . . because he needs to clear the decks for an inverse strategy of sacralization which will messianize the Cause of the Equals'.[3] There have been the expected references to the Revolution as a 'text', between the covers of which, let the social and human fact be noted, hundreds of thousands of human beings were killed. This is not to argue that words, language, rhetoric, do not carry perhaps extraordinary weight in times of revolution. Revolutions must not only be done; they must be seen and heard to be done. Thus, during the 1790s, place-names and christian names had to be altered – rue Voltaire for the rue des vierges, Ile de la Fraternité for the Ile Saint-Louis, Jean-Jacques for Joseph etc. – not once but several times, depending on the political situation. But to argue that 'In the beginning was the word and the word was with the Revolution' is to distort historical reality in much the same way as the 'more vulgar econometric marxist was accused of doing a couple of decades ago.

The study of semiotics – the 'language' of signs and symbols – has certainly deepened our understanding of the revolutionary phenomenon when handled in a sensible and balanced fashion. Historians such as Lynn Hunt and James Leith have done just this. Despite the fact that Professor Hunt is prone to become a little too intoxicated with 'the psycho-symbolics of the revolutionary political imagination' at times,[4] her conclusion to an analysis of 'The Imagery of Radicalism' that 'the representations of revolution gave definition to the experience of power' is not only intelligent, but intelligible. James Leith's recent *Space and Revolution* contains many references to the importance of signs, symbols, statues and monuments, and we shall return to his work. Let us simply note at this point that both of the above scholars provide useful bridges to carry us over the gulf that left- and right-wing ideologues have sought to create between *marxisant* and revisionist interpretations of the Revolution. Lynn Hunt has argued that 'The revolutionary political class can be termed bourgeois *both in terms of social position and of class consciousness* (my italics)', but, in order to underline the importance of the cultural framework within which the bourgeoisie operated, draws our attention to the importance of their cultural formation, their 'language and imagery'.[5] Patrice Higonnet offers a more universalist interpretation of the cultural significance of the bourgeois revolution 'a genuinely progressive moment in world history, a moment whose meaning transcends both the collapse of the monarchy and the substitution of merit and wealth to birth and caste as the organizing principles of western culture'.[6]

However, there is a powerful case for the argument that the most profound cultural shift which occurred during the second half of the eighteenth century was not always translated into words, and had more to do with attitudes to life and death rather than to linguistics, or, to put this in fashionable semiotic language, the sign of the cross was the most potent symbol of the *ancien régime*. Professor McManners has noted that, as life expectancy increased, death did not exercise the same dominion over the thoughts of the French as the Revolution approached, and that this transformed human relationships, on several levels:

> With a longer time together, affections could more often deepen and diversify. At the same time, the old community and neighbourhood life was beginning to disintegrate; guilds, the village youth organisations, kinship groups, the nexus of conformity around the parish church would exercise less power over young people's minds.[7]

The demographic, sociological, economic and associated psychological changes of the post-1750s period may well hold the key to the derivation of the most over-worked word in the revisionist revolutionary lexicon, *régénération*. The top priority for the political and cultural elite of the French Revolution was the creation of *'l'homme nouveau'*, a new Adam (Eve would follow him) re-housed in a secularised, rationalised Garden of Eden. Rousseau had created the prototype with his *Emile*, that horribly precocious child of the marriage between intellect and emotion. To create their new man, the Revolution would have to begin with the 'regeneration' of the Catholic Church.

On the eve of the Revolution, 'For that 82 per cent of French men and women who lived in the countryside the practice of the Catholic religion was a central and unquestioned part of their existence.'[8] One of the crucial cultural facts of our period is the attempt to replace the ubiquitous influence of the Catholic Church, inextricably linked to the structures of a dying feudal society, with a more rational, utilitarian form of religion. The most revolutionary event of the 1790s, as Alphonse Aulard pointed out a century ago, was the introduction in 1793 of the revolutionary Calendar. The new world which was to be inhabited by the new man would now begin with the birth of the Republic, not with the birth of Christ. 'Revolutionary Man' would be secularised from birth; that event, like his marriage and death, would henceforth be recorded, in revolutionary days, months and years, in the registers of the town hall, not in the Gregorian divisions of time employed in his parish church. The real radicalism of the French Revolution arose from its challenge to the spiritual life of the French people, and it could be argued that its failure was more evident in the spiritual than in the social realm. Marxist historiography of the Revolution, naturally orientated towards the market rather than the Catholic mass, tends to under-estimate the significance of the psycho-spiritual.

There is, it is true, compelling evidence to support the argument that religion was losing the battle to control the hearts and minds of the French people long before 1789. Whether we take wills and the reduction in the number of masses to be said after death, declining interest in the priesthood as a vocation, the even sharper loss of interest in the monastic life, many more French men and women were becoming more concerned with life before, rather than after death. There were very interesting regional differences and it is noticeable that women continued to be attracted to the 'caring professions' still controlled by the Church, but the general trend is unmistakable. The attack upon the Catholic Church was, of course, a central plank in the programme of the Enlightenment, its more radical wing espousing atheistical doctrines. Condillac's materialist, even mechanistic philosophy led him to argue, to Rousseau's horror, that man was little more than a collection of atoms, a view shared by some contemporary philosophers such as Professor Daniel Dennett who sees man as a 'sophisticated biological mechanism' and computers as capable of developing 'consciousness'. But the main thrust of the Enlightenment and enlightened thinking on religion was utilitarian, an attempt to reinterpret the Bible in the light of reason. Atheism was something to be practised by consenting intellectuals in the privacy of their own salons.

D'Alembert, joint editor of the *Encyclopédie*, had summed it all up decades before the Revolution when he criticised theologians for elevating their personal opinions into universal dogma. According to d'Alembert, religion was intended 'uniquely to regulate our mode of life and our faith; they believed it was to enlighten us also with the system of the world'.[9] Yet another interesting division of labour – priests should be concerned with morals and mortality; philosophers with telling us how society should be organised. But theses were being advanced which were revolutionising man's understanding of time as well as of his place in the order of things. J-B. Lamarck's work on 'biological transformism' foreshadowed the evolutionary theories of Charles Darwin. In his influential work, *Histoire naturelle*, the comte de Buffon undermined the traditional view of man as being made in the image of God when he wrote: 'The first truth which issues from this serious examination of nature is a truth which perhaps humbles man. This truth is that he ought to classify himself with the animals.'[10] For the time, this was a truly revolutionary statement. The fact that, in common with Newton, Buffon stressed that the wonders of nature only confirmed the existence of a Deity did little to sugar the all too rational pill.

The religious programme of the Revolution, which sought to rebaptise the French people in the waters of science and rationalism, was founded upon the intellectual revolution of the eighteenth century, as well as on the popular disenchantment with the Church which was far more socio-economic in substance. Certainly the 'nationalisation' of Church lands in November 1789 was prompted by the need to pay off the debts of the State, but it would be quite wrong to ignore the profound shift in elite and popular opinion which provided the sanction for this revolutionary, and fateful, move. Placing the lands of the Church at the disposal of the nation, stripping the Church of its income through the tithe (representing a sum of around 100 million *livres*), forbidding the taking of monastic vows (13 February 1790), all this represented the end of a phase in the history of western, Catholic civilisation. The Civil Constitution of the Clergy, passed on 12 July 1790, represented the culmination of this religious revolution. Many of its provisions could be swallowed by those clerics who had involved themselves in the pre-revolutionary debates on the need for change: increased payment to the lower clergy, the attack on non-residence, the reduction in the number of minor religious posts, even the new 'Gallican' relationship with the papacy. However, the abolition of all archbishoprics as well as fifty bishoprics helps to explain why the upper clergy found the Civil Constitution distinctly unpalatable, whilst the introduction of popular elections for bishops and *curés* stuck in the throat of most Catholics.

None the less, there is considerable truth in Timothy Tackett's conclusion that it was not so much the Civil Constitution of the Clergy itself, but the requirement, on 27 November 1790, that the clergy should swear an oath of allegiance to the Constitution that turned a crisis into a disaster. After all, the pope himself did not denounce the Constitution until the following spring. Only seven out of 160 bishops took the oath; just over half of the lower clergy did so. As we have seen, the counter-revolution would receive a major boost out of the religious discord of 1790, particularly from the legislation imprisoning and exiling non-juring clergy. Ralph Gibson, agreeing with Tackett that the crisis over the oath to the Civil Constitution of the Clergy was a 'seminal event', stresses that 'it was also the crystallisation of a pre-existing geography of religious fervour'.[11] Tackett's conclusions include the point that final decisions were linked to 'broader cultural assumptions and opinions of fellow citizens and fellow clergymen across whole *pays* or provinces'. In parts of the west, like the Morbihan, 90 per cent of the clergy rejected the Constitution; in parts of the south-east, like the Var, 90 per cent voted in favour. Tackett is uncertain whether or not one should describe this very complex crisis as a 'cultural revolution'; he is certain that the 'mental topography of French society would never be the same again'.[12]

If the religious crisis of the opening years of the Revolution was provoked by 'cultural', as well as by socio-economic factors – relationships between the *curé* and his flock, the contiguity of Protestant and Catholic communities, communities which did not speak French, the problem of land tenure and the payment of the tithe – war transformed problems of faith into ideological confrontations. Only a few weeks after the declaration of war with Austria on 20 April 1792, the king further alienated himself from prevailing political opinion when he vetoed a draconian law which stated that any priest could be deported on the denunciation of twenty citizens. By the end of the revolutionary decade, over 30,000 priests would be forced to leave France, many for good; several thousands who remained were executed: 'The 1790s . . . established a barrier between supporters of the Church and supporters of the Revolution that would dominate French politics until at least the First World War.'[13] However, the brief, and politically disastrous, dechristianisation campaign during the autumn and winter of 1793–4 was – and still is – regarded by many militants as the final stage in the creation of the new revolutionary man. The poet Chénier teamed up with the composer Gossec to compose his anthem, the 'Hymn to Liberty', for the ceremony on 10 November 1793 when the cathedral of Notre-Dame was rededicated to the worship of Reason. From an elitist standpoint, dechristianisation can legitimately be viewed as the logical outcome of the materialist philosophy of the Enlightenment; so far as popular culture is concerned, it was an explosion of popular sentiment against the moralising wing of the post-Tridentine clergy, unleashed by the critical political circumstances of the period.

What is certain is that politicians such as Robespierre and Danton did not like it, not just because it was politically inexpedient, which it was, but because it ran counter to the main current of Enlightenment thought noted above – that Catholicism, as practised by its clergy, was undoubtedly built upon the sands of 'feudal' superstition and intolerance, but that faith in a 'Supreme Being', whether Newton's Clockmaker, Buffon's Creator of the Species, or the Freemason's 'Architect of the Universe', was right and proper. It has often been said that the famous Law of 14 *frimaire* Year II/4 December 1793 centralising government in the hands of the Committee of Public Safety is one of the most important pieces of legislation to be passed during the 1790s, but, from the standpoint of the spiritual and cultural lives of the mass of French men and women, the decree confirming the principle of the freedom of worship, passed just two days later, was equally, if not more important. Robespierre's attitude towards religion remained fairly consistent and was summed up in his remarkable, universalist speech in support of the decree introducing the cult of the Supreme Being on 18 *floréal* Year II/7 May 1794. Noting that 'One half of the world revolution is already achieved, the other half has yet to be accomplished', Robespierre explained that 'The real priest of the Supreme Being is Nature; . . . His festivals, the joy of a great people gathered together beneath His eyes in order to draw close the sweet bonds of universal brotherhood and offer Him the homage of pure and feeling hearts. . . .'[14] One can hear Rousseau breathing 'Amen' to this!

And Robespierre was not alone. Throughout the period of the Directory, and well into Napoleon's reign, the anti-clericalism inherited from the eighteenth century and sharpened by the events of the Revolution continued to dictate government policy. On 3 *ventôse* Year III/21 February 1795, the revolutionary Church child of the Civil Constitution of the Clergy was formally separated from the State and public worship permitted in private houses. Following the *coup* of 18 *fructidor* Year V/4 September 1797, a new, and vicious, wave of repression was launched against the non-juring clergy. The politics of war and counter-revolution continued to refashion the religious and cultural life of France until Napoleon's Concordat tied up some of the loose ends in 1802. The Deist policies of the Directory, with *fêtes* organised for practically everything from the cradle to the grave, failed to win over the mass of the people; indeed, as Olwen Hufton has shown, popular Catholicism, with women in the vanguard, emerged from the Terror and the Directory bloody but distinctly unbowed.[15] None the less, the Revolution had profoundly altered the cultural life of France: 'the quasi-universal (religious) practice of the *ancien régime* would never be re-established'.[16]

If *l'homme nouveau* was to be created, *ab initio*, in the revolutionary church, the schoolroom was to be the second station on the revolutionary cross. For Mona Ozouf, schools were central to 'the discourse of regeneration' which was, for her, 'a pedagogical discourse and all the revolutionaries invested the educational issue with enormous symbolic significance'.[17] The Constituent Assembly was too busy with the momentous problems of reshaping the constitutional, religious and economic affairs of the nation to deal at length with education, but its successor, the Legislative Assembly, created a Committee on Public Instruction under the chairmanship of the 'last of the *philosophes*', Condorcet. His project, presented to the Assembly just as war was being declared, was far too voluntary, elitist, not to say idealistic, for the increasingly radical and egalitarian times. In August, teaching orders like the Oratorians would be dissolved. Lepeletier de Saint-Fargeau's project, supported by Robespierre, offered an equally impractical, but sharply contrasting vision, of education completely controlled by the State, positively Spartan in its methods and aims. A compromise appears to have been reached with Bouquier's project which was passed by the Convention on 29 *frimaire* Year II/19 December 1793. Building upon the law of 30 May 1793, it provided for a compulsory national system of education at the primary level, but allowed private schools to operate, under the tutelage of the State. The syllabus was to be 'modern', with an emphasis upon science, mathematics, modern languages, religious indoctrination being replaced with the inculcation of solid, civic and republican virtues.

Once again, studying the Revolution from the angle of cultural history, Thermidor represents a significant change of direction, towards a more practical, elitist policy, but, a policy which continues to challenge the influence of the Church, at least in the sphere of higher education. As early as 27 *brumaire* Year III/17 November 1794, primary education was made voluntary; education policy would now be focused far more on the secondary and tertiary sectors. The Daunou legisation of 3 *brumaire* Year IV/25 October 1795 laid down the framework – support for the establishment of the *grandes écoles*, like the *Ecole Polytechnique*, still one of the most prestigious and elitist institutions in France; the creation of the secondary *écoles centrales* (forerunners of today's *lycées*) to produce, from the sons of the elite, the cadres for the new State; some provision for the education of the female sex. We have here the prototype of the two-tier system of education which characterised French education, certainly until the 1950s: one level for the popular masses, another for the elites; the continuing dual system of State-run lay schools alongside private, mainly Catholic *collèges*, with the difference that, increasingly after 1794, primary education, at least until Guizot's law of 1833, would be left almost entirely to the religious teaching orders. In education, as in politics, the Revolution would move towards the establishment of an elitist, essentially bourgeois solution. We use the word 'prototype', because, again due to lack of time and funds, most of the educational policies of the Revolution remained on the drawing board. William Doyle goes so far as to say that the Revolution 'created chaos in education, and a marked drop in numbers undergoing it'.[18]

The determination of a revolutionary elite to recreate the French people in their own image is one of the main theses propounded by

Carla Hesse in her recent work on the Press and publishing in Paris during the 1790s. However, as in the sphere of education, revolutionary time and circumstance, aggravated by the introduction of free-market capitalist ideas, raised insuperable problems for influential policy-makers such as the *abbé* Grégoire, intent upon bridging the gap not only between *ancien régime* and revolutionary versions of Catholicism, but, more generally, between elite and popular cultures. The importance of the Press was noted in an earlier chapter. A related expansion in printing and publishing was evident during the 1790s: in 1789, 36 printer/publishers and 194 publisher/booksellers were at work in the capital; a decade later, the number of printing and publishing outlets had tripled. The first 'Press Barons' were born. Charles Panckoucke, first editor of the *Moniteur* owned twenty-seven presses and employed, at the peak of his power, over 800 workers. However, our interest is not so much in the growth of the industry as in its contribution to the maturation of *l'homme nouveau*. Hesse's work relates the changing function of the Press and publishing during the Revolution to the new legal and institutional framework created after 1789, insisting that what we are dealing with is a cultural revolution created by the 'cultural politics' of the 1790s.

In the first place, the abolition of the *ancien régime* Administration of the Book Trade, responsible for official censorship, as well as the Paris Book Guild, which had protected the interests of printers, created new and dangerous possibilities for the freedom to speak, write and publish, particularly with the onset of war and counter-revolution. The immediate impact of the 'free market in ideas' which the Revolution produced had been an economic collapse, prompting the more established printers and publishers, like Panckoucke, to demand the setting-up of a more open version of the old Paris Book Guild. But, 'The economic crisis in the guild was . . . a symptom of cultural revolution.'[19] The concept of the 'author' was being transformed from that of a clerk for the transmission of ideas handed down from God, or even, as Condorcet favoured, that of a channel for the communication of ideas which were universal and social in origin, to the notion – more congenial to Diderot – that ideas were 'individual', the product of individual genius. In other words, the Revolution gave birth to, if it did not conceive of, the 'bourgeois author'. The law of 19 July 1793 gave legal recognition to this development, granting authors rights to their works during their lifetime and to their heirs for ten years after their death (Napoleon would subsequently double this *post-mortem* privilege). Then there was the exploitation of the Press for overtly political and revolutionary purposes, a practice not unknown during the *ancien régime* but usually carried out underground or abroad. From 1789, the cheap wooden presses of the period worked overtime to satisfy the insatiable demand for 'news'. Apart from the well-known examples of Hébert's *Pére Duchesne* and Desmoulin's *Vieux Cordelier*, there were the sectionary militants such as Antoine-François Momoro, printer-by-appointment to the Cordelier Club, and the Girondist members of the *Cercle Social* which printed 180 books, newspapers, and pamphlets, including Tom Paine's *Rights of Man*, between 1791 and 1793. As the Revolution entered a more violent and radical phase after the spring of 1792, publishing political material became an extremely dangerous pastime: Hébert, Desmoulins and Momoro all ended up as victims of madame guillotine.

For governments, increasingly concerned with the development of popular politics, the destabilising consequences of a free Press and individual authorial rights posed problems. Early discussion of the latter had occurred within the context of a debate on sedition and libel. Once again, defenders of censorship fell back upon the tried and tested formula that freedom of the Press did not mean a licence to attack those who were responsible for the well-being of the State. Gradually, governments, from the Jacobin to the Napoleonic, would bring all official printing under their direct control. Napoleon would re-introduce censorship and a reduction in the number of newspapers officially allowed to circulate in France. But there was a further complication, one that went to the heart of the cultural agenda of the revolutionary elite. For the most representative of its members, such as the *abbé* Grégoire and the editor of the *Feuille Villageoise*, Pierre-Louis Guinguené, democratic access to France's cultural heritage was crucial to the creation of *l'homme nouveau*, but that heritage had to be purged of its religious, licentious, and 'politically incorrect' components. Unfortunately, the free market encouraged the republication and wider circulation of matters pertaining to sex rather than to the Social Contract. For Carla Hesse, Grégoire's report of 17 *vendémiaire* Year III/5 October 1794 represents a 'cultural Thermidor'. Advocating a policy of raising the cultural and political consciousness of the nation, Grégoire encouraged the granting of subventions to authors and publishers who thought upon the 'right' cultural and political lines. During the Directory, the government would, in fact, dole out millions of *livres* in grants to favoured sons. All to little avail as we shall see.

Move into the public sphere of architecture and we find this same concern for the creation of a new cultural order, for a new physical environment suitable for the new revolutionary man. James Leith informs us that 'belief in the possibility of creating a *nouvel homme* lay behind the cultural programs of the Revolution'.[20] The 361 illustrations of plans for monuments, buildings and festivals contained in Leith's *Space and Revolution* suggest that the revolutionary dream of a new Athens was nothing short of grandiose. Look at Etienne Boullée's drawings for his immense coliseum, part of his plans for a new public space on the Champs Elysées; Pierre Rousseau's designs for the complete redevelopment of the Ecole des Beaux Arts *quartier*; 'the strange and powerful' project conceived by François Verly for a new city centre in Lille, complete with adjacent 'male' and 'female' columns and domes. All of them foreshadow the architectural arrogance that the two Napoleons, I and III, would impose upon *le vieux Paris*. However, what strikes one most forcibly is the lack of originality and creative innovation, antiquity exercising a powerful influence over artists and architects alike. Verly's columns, *agoras*, complete with public baths, do offer a hint of 'modernism', but, in general, the Doric column, the obelisk and the rotunda win hands down. The work of Boullée, Ledoux and Lequeu emphasise the point that the cultural shift from the rococo to the neo-classical was in intellectual harmony with the 'rational', physical universe created by the Enlightenment.

Once again, political instability, war and financial constraints provide the main explanations for the pathetic physical legacy of the revolutionary era. It is ironic that the French Revolution, whose impact was felt world-wide, should have left so little material evidence of its existence. However, it would be quite wrong to dismiss this aspect of the cultural history of the Revolution as devoid of meaning. There were, for example, the 127 paintings, the plans for 110 sculptures, and the 195 architectural projects submitted for the National Competition of the Year II, at the very peak of the Terror, in fact. These represent just a part of the artistic and cultural legacy of the Revolution. However, as was the case with the printed word, 'the *concours* of the Year II failed utterly to produce the works of propaganda for which the government of the Year II had hoped'.[21] There is something peculiarly satisfying in this failure on the part of the revolutionary elite to harness genius to the chariot-wheels of the State.

There was, of course, one outstanding figure who was prepared, indeed eager, to allow his genius to be harnessed – Jacques-Louis David. For David, the Revolution offered the opportunity, not only of artistic regeneration, of emancipation from the stultifying influence of the royal *Académie* which, at one painful stage of his career, had driven him to contemplate suicide, but also of contributing to the cultural formation of a nation. He wrote, at the time he was preparing his sketches for his unfinished painting of the Tennis-Court Oath (revolutionary time moved too fast, even for David!): 'French Nation! It is your glory that I wish to propagate', adding that the same offer was available to the 'Peuples de l'Univers, présents et futurs'.[22] From the beginning, David was attracted to the radical wing of the Revolution. He courted the company of the Jacobins, of Robespierre, even Marat. His famous painting of the martyred Marat combines his personal sense of loss with the romance of revolution and the simplicity of neo-classical art. Diderot would have loved it. During the Terror, he became a member of the Committee of General Security and, although his expiatory year in prison after Thermidor altered his perspective on art and politics, it did not eradicate his sympathy for the more extreme revolutionaries. He would be one of the few subscribers to Babeuf's *Tribun du Peuple*.

David's contribution to the culture and politics of the Revolution was not, of course, limited to painting. Since his father died when he was young and his mother appears not to have doted upon him, the young Jacques-Louis was brought up by two uncles, both architects (one of my own favourite paintings of David is that of his aunt, madame Buron, which is almost 'impressionist' in tone). James Leith notes that David involved himself in the plans of many architectural projects during the Revolution, particularly those drawn up by Verly in the latter's designs for the rebuilding of the city centre of Lille. David also designed costumes for the *représentants de la nation*.[23] But, apart from this and, of course, his paintings which span one of the most turbulent half-centuries in French history and which represent a watershed in the history of European art, David was also the 'Pageant-Master of the Republic'. The revolutionary festivals were, perhaps, the most successful of the many attempts to imprint the message of the Revolution upon the hearts and minds of the French people. Modifed and transformed to suit local cultures, the *fête* involved ordinary people in the drama of the Revolution. For Mona Ozouf, the festivals transferred the sacrality associated with the religious culture of the *ancien régime* on to the political and social plane.[24] The *fête* was the cultural cradle for many a revolutionary *homme nouveau*. And not only for *l'homme nouveau* this time; women played a far more prominent part in the festivals than in any other comparable manifestation of revolutionary political culture.

Let us take just two of the *fêtes* master-minded by David to explain what kind of cultural and political message the leaders of the

Revolution wished to convey – *the fête de l'Unité et l'Indivisibilité* held on 10 August 1793 and the *fête de l'Etre Suprême,* 20 *prairial* Year II/ 8 June 1794. The first provides convincing proof of the validity of Mona Ozouf's thesis concerning the transference of sacrality from the religious to the secular in a very obvious way. During the festival, the procession was scheduled to stop at five points, imitating the Stations of the Cross. Onlookers were asked to 'worship' at the shrines of Nature and Liberty, the fountains of 'Regeneration', as well as to recall the great political events of the Revolution. At one station 'In front of the goddess a huge pile of feudal charters, coats of arms, and other emblems of the Old Regime had been amassed.' The symbol at the fourth station was a mountain, a reference both to the Jacobins who sat on the high benches in the Convention as well as to the legendary and symbolic significance of mountains.[25] If the message was 'modern', including an appeal to defeat the federalist movement which had just erupted in the provinces, the imagery was 'ancient' – columns, obelisks, statues of Hercules dominated the eye. Again, for the *fête de l'Etre Suprême,* huge columns and volcanic mountains overawed the spectators. Lynn Hunt makes the interesting observation that if we compare the representation of Hercules used at this *fête,* composed and classical in demeanour, with the rugged and brutal figure used for the 10 August festival, we see the political evolution of the Revolution from its popular phase in 1793 to its more conventional, *étatiste* phase in the summer of the following year: 'The people in the meantime had been brought under control.'[26]

It is certainly true that, following the downfall of the Jacobins, indeed, from the winter of 1793-4, the revolutionary elite made a determined and successful attempt to exclude the popular masses from the political scene. The Thermidorean reaction not only encompassed the final collapse of the Popular Movement, it unleashed a popular counter-revolution which would ultimately push the wealthy group which ran the Directory into an even more elitist stance. As Carla Hesse pointed out there was a 'cultural Thermidor' which reflected the failure of the revolutionary elite to embrace the entire nation within its chill, marble, neo-classical embrace.

One can trace the failure in virtually every sphere of cultural activity discussed above. In the religious field, by 1795, the Thermidoreans had given up any meaningful attempt to eradicate the old Catholic faith, leaving people to their own spiritual devices. Robespierre's attempt through the cult of the Supreme Being to create 'a popular God, a God of the people' ended in the intellectual cul-de-sac of Theophilanthropy,

David being one of its devotees. In the field of education, the children of the lower orders were returned to the Catholic fold and the indoctrination of the Brothers of the Christian Life whilst those of the notables went on to higher things in the *écoles centrales* and the *grandes écoles*. France was well on the road from an aristocratic to a bourgeois meritocratic society. Its members would purchase the beautifully bound volumes produced by publishers such as Pierre Didot *ainé*. The increasingly literate masses (two-thirds of the population by the beginning of the nineteenth century) would enjoy the increasing flow of cheap novels, like the best-seller *Victor ou l'enfant de la forêt* by Ducray-Duminil. Almanacs and anti-clerical stories would continue to rub spines in the *colporteur*'s sack with the Lives of the Saints, although political tracts would become much more common. In the theatre, Monvel's *Les Victimes cloitrées*, complete with lustful monks and beautiful maidens, would fill the *Comédie* in place of Pierre-Sylvain Maréchal's political extravaganza *Le Jugement dernier des rois*.[27] Even the symbolic representations chosen by the elites were all Greek to the masses. As Lynn Hunt notes, Hercules was 'the artist–intellectual–politician's image of the people for the people's edification'.[28] Hébert's foul-mouthed, pipe-smoking *Père Duchesne* had awakened a far more positive response from the reader in the Clamart *cabaret*.

Benjamin Constant arrived in Paris just as the sansculotte uprisings of the spring of 1795 were being crushed. Events such as these must have convinced the youthful lover of Madame de Staël of the futility of the fraternal, universalist dreams of 1789. He, more than any other contemporary political commentator, went to the heart of the matter, to the heart of the intellectual and cultural failure of the Revolution – the failure to grasp the reality of the times. For Constant, politics was the art of understanding the nature of the present, not reinterpreting that of the past: 'Those involved commonly fail to grasp the true nature of the moment and the true constraints on their action.'[29] In other words, it was time, as Karl Marx himself would argue, for the revolutionary elite to cast away their togas; only then could the frock-coated nineteenth-century bourgeois lurking beneath be identified. There is clearly a great deal of common sense, that cautious child of hindsight, in such observations. But, from another angle of vision, Thermidor steered the Revolution back to its intellectual – as opposed to its socio-economic – mooring, to that elitist, cultured *quai* of the Enlightenment which excluded all popular craft. The group known as the *Idéologues* would temper Enlightenment thought with the experience of the Terror to produce the intellectual, socially conservative, liberalism of François Guizot. Bronislav Baczko is probably right to conclude that, for the narrow cultural elite of 1795, 'The Revolution began with the Enlightenment, to end it, one had to return to the Enlightenment.'[30] For the *philosophe*, as for the *Idéologue*, the lower orders were to be forced to accept only a supporting role in the drama of history.

Conclusion

The French Revolution is the historical event which has launched a thousand *colloques*. Contemporaries knew that it would. For William Wordsworth, recalling his visit to France in 1791–2:

> 'The land all swarmed with passion, like a Plain
> Devour'd by locusts, Carra, Gorsas, add
> A hundred other names, forgotten now,
> Nor to be heard of more, yet were they Powers,
> Like earthquakes, shocks repeated day by day,
> And felt through every nook of town and field.'[1]

At the height of the Terror, Maximilien Robespierre expressed the opinion that 'The French people appear to have outstripped the rest of the human race by two thousand years'.[2] Karl Marx was not wholly convinced, criticising the tendency of the French bourgeoisie to go back 2,000 years and dress up in Roman togas, but then Karl Marx was German, not French. None the less, the marxist interpretation of history, which placed the French Revolution in a dynamic, world-historical perspective, helps to explain the continued fascination – and repulsion – of the revolutionary period for generations of historians. Immanuel Wallerstein argues that 'the French Revolution and its Napoleonic continuation catalyzed the ideological transformation of the capitalist world-economy *as a world-system*'.[3] Even revisionist historians, who deny the transforming power of the Revolution in the process of capitalist change, agree that, from a political and cultural angle of vision, the events of the Revolution 'have since become the basic script for the modern drama of "revolution" still central to the meaning of politics in our own century'.[4]

Marxisant historians have prioritised the socio-economic interpretation of the Revolution, revisionists the politico-cultural; there appears to be little chance of a meeting of minds. But before we hazard a few opinions on the possible emergence of a 'post-revisionist' consensus, let us examine, perforce very briefly, divisions *within* the ranks of *marxisant* and revisionist historians in an attempt to establish the fact that what divides the two camps *may* not be as important as that which unites them. Let us begin with the central issues of capitalism and class.

One of Professor Cobban's principal objections to the marxist 'social' interpretation of the Revolution was that if '1789' was a 'bourgeois revolution', it was certainly not precipitated by an industrial, capitalist bourgeoisie, since capitalism before 1789 was still, in the main, commercial and proprietary. Most revisionist historians have followed this lead – if '1789' was a 'bourgeois revolution', it was certainly not a *capitalist*, bourgeois revolution, one which laid the foundations of a modern, industrialised society. France was predominantly an agrarian society; factories were few and far between; traditional, *commercial*, not industrial, capitalism held sway, and so on. However, agreement on this central issue is certainly not unanimous amongst the revisionists. As we have seen, it was a leading revisionist historian, Guy Chaussinand-Nogaret, who argued that France, *before 1789*, experienced an industrial 'take-off', 'an industrialised France would be born from the old regime experiments that Le Creusot or the cotton industries managed to keep going'.[5] Not all revisionists, therefore, are obsessed by rhetoric and semiotics; a few offer important, new interpretations concerning the development of modern capitalism. Nor should it be thought that all *marxisant* historians favour the idea of a fully fledged, industrial, capitalist bourgeoisie precipitating a revolutionary crisis. For example, it is somewhat ironic that Albert Soboul, a constant target of revisionist historians, condemned out of hand as a 'marxist-leninist' ideologue, should have painted a far less rosy picture of industrial growth in France before the Revolution than did Chaussinand-Nogaret, repeatedly reminding us that 'Capitalism [before 1789] was still essentially commercial.'[6] For Soboul, as for many other marxist historians, the real crisis of the *ancien régime* concerns the *retardation* of modern forms of capitalist production, blocked by the structures and *mentalités* of an aristocratic society. The significance of 1789 was that many, though not all, of these blockages were removed.

There remains, however, a fundamental difference in approach, indeed, I would argue, *the* fundamental difference in approach between *marxisant* and revisionist historians. This concerns questions of class and revolution, the role of *necessary*, possibly violent, class struggle in the process of historical change. Was an 'elite' of bourgeois and nobles responsible for promoting capitalist growth, or was there a necessary, predetermined, historic clash between a 'capitalist' bourgeois class and a 'feudal' noble class? For Chaussinand-Nogaret capitalism was associated with an elite, an elite led, however, by the nobility, not the bourgeoisie. For Albert Soboul, on the other hand, the link between the bourgeoisie and the evolution of modern capitalism is central to his *social*, class, interpretation of history. The opening sentence of his impressive general work on the Revolution is uncompromising: 'The Revolution of 1789–94 marked the arrival of modern bourgeois capitalist society in the history of France.'[7] For Soboul, for what he termed 'the classic historiographical tradition' (i.e. *marxisant*) of the French Revolution, '1789' was a necessary stage in the development of a modern, bourgeois, capitalist society, just as 1917 and 1949 represented stages in the realisation of the marxist utopia of a communist, then classless society. The conservative culture of the 1970s and 1980s in America and Britain, the fall of Stalinist, communist regimes in Europe altered the historical agenda, creating more politico-cultural space for revisionist approaches to the Revolution, and to history in general.

But, to return to this possibility of the emergence of a post-revisionist consensus, it should be noted that, long before the fall of the Berlin Wall, *marxisant* historians were moving to accommodate the valid criticisms of revisionists concerned about too determinist, too structuralist an approach to the study of history. Edward Thompson's aptly titled work, *The Poverty of Theory*, a powerful indictment of Althusserian, ahistorical structuralism, containing a few side-swipes at Marx himself (no wonder Thompson has often been regarded by true believers as more of an English Whig historian than a marxist!) was published as early as 1978. Eight years before this, Régine Robin produced a study of the social structure of Semur-en-Auxois which argued, *inter alia*, that the period we are dealing with should be seen as a 'transitional' one in the process of change between a feudal and capitalist society.[8] For Robin, the actions and attitudes of the pre-revolutionary bourgeoisie were conditioned by their place in a post-feudal society, a unique, transitional society, but one in which capitalism was undermining the old feudal structures. Robin's thesis posits a less rigid separation between a 'capitalist' and a 'feudal' mode of production, thus satisfying part, at least, of the revisionist case. It knocks a big hole in the more rigid, class-conflict theories of historical change. As Tim Blanning explains: 'Such a pattern is entirely compatible with Marxist theory and, ironically, can accommodate without strain the empirical research of revisionists seeking to deny the validity of that theory.'[9] I should like to see more research conducted along the lines suggested by Robin, and more particularly by Cristopher Johnson concentrating, in particular, on the relationship between proto-industrialisation, changing patterns of work, and the social consequences of these changes. [10] If eighteenth-century French society was a transitional, *unique* form of society, the essential bridge to the fully developed capitalist society of the nineteenth century, then proto-industrial structures, which could and did accommodate seigneurial interests, may be said to have provided the central arches.

More recently, George Comninel produced an interesting and provocative book entitled *Rethinking the French Revolution: Marxism and the Revisionist Challenge*, which went much further than Robin's in its acceptance – very uncritically in places – of the revisionist argument concerning the lack of modern capitalist development before 1789, but endeavouring to retain an 'historical materialist' approach to the problems this posed for a *marxisant* sociologist. Comninel's book is long on theory and short on facts, but it illustrates the lengths to which, in this post-modern, post-communist age, marxist thinkers are prepared to go to meet the revisionist challenge. For Comninel, as for Edward Thompson to a certain extent, Marx himself was long on theory and short on facts. He argues with some conviction, that Marx never really studied the pre-revolutionary period in France; he simply borrowed the notion of the 'bourgeois revolution' from the French early nineteenth-century historians such as François Guizot. There can be no doubt that the identification between the 'triumph of the bourgeoisie' and the French Revolution had been made long before Marx. Sieyès and Barnave had laid the foundations for the thesis during the Revolution itself, whilst it was François Mignet, not Karl Marx, who wrote: 'The Fourteenth of July had been the triumph of the middle class.'[11]

However, according to Comninel, the Barnaves, the Guizots and the Mignets were wrong, and hence so was Marx, since he did little more than borrow the idea from them. Anyway, for historians like Mignet and Guizot, history was certainly not a process; it stopped with the arrival of the all-conquering bourgeoisie in 1830. Interesting that the American revisionist Francis Fukuyama should have convinced himself that the 'The End of History' should be dated from America's victory over the Soviet Union in the 1980s – yet another attempt to suggest that liberal capitalism is the answer to western Europe's prayers. Comninel is convinced that the revolutionary bourgeoisie did not simply represent 'a capitalist class'; furthermore, that there was 'no fundamental social division between the forms of property and economic interests of the bourgeoisie and the nobility'.[12] Here surely is another bridge across the troubled waters of *marxisant* and revisionist historiography. There was no 'class struggle' related to the growth of modern forms of capitalism before, or indeed during, the Revolution; there was, instead, conflict within a ruling elite.

Is the similarity, however, more apparent than real? Was 'the Revolution simply a political contest between rival factions of a single "elite" ', Comninel asks. His answer, an unequivocal 'Of course not', suggests that the two sides are continuing to shout at each other over a pretty wide chasm. For Comninel, after all, 'The French Revolution was a specific product of the class relations of the ancien régime.' 'Class struggle' is very much back on the agenda. In pre-revolutionary France, peasants, among other social groups, were being exploited, and 'Recognition of the fundamental exploitative relationship is necessarily also recognition of class struggle.' However, it should be noted that these class struggles are not related directly to the existence of modern forms of capitalism before 1789, nor to the exploitation of a non-existent 'proletariat', nor to the 'feudal' exploitation of the peasantry, since 'feudalism' too was, in Comninel's mistaken view, the fiction of vulgar marxist historians. The class struggles of the *ancien régime* were created out of the conflict between 'bourgeois' and 'aristocrat' over the spoils (surplus-value in marxist parlance) to be acquired from the State which, following the line taken by de Tocqueville, had become the supreme arbitrator of power, social and political. For Comninel, class exploitation is as much political as it is economic. Stripped of its marxist rhetoric, there is surely much in Comninel's interpretation which reminds one of the influential article published by Colin Lucas in 1973, 'Nobles, bourgeois and the origins of the French Revolution',[13] including the idea of a 'section of the ruling class', and 'an intra-class conflict over basic political relations' with an aristocratic elite elbowing aside an aspiring but thwarted bourgeoisie 'interested in a state administration open to talent'.

There is a final point concerning the possibility, if not – dare I phrase it thus? – of a synthesis emerging from the dialectical struggle between *marxisant* and revisionist historians, then of some measure of agreement (only totalitarian ideologues would ask for more!) over the meaning of the Revolution two hundred years on. It is interesting, for example, that two historians, approaching the same problem from very different methodological perspectives, should both conclude that not enough emphasis has been placed on the importance of the State when studying both the causes and the course of the French Revolution. For Comninel, aspiring bourgeois and the higher echelons of the aristocracy were competing for power which was mediated through the State. The *political* crisis of 1787–9, when the bourgeoisie realised that the aristocracy was intent on seizing greater control over the State and, in consequence, made a take-over bid for *la nation*, was also economic, since the State was 'intimately involved', through legal and political channels, in the process of economic exploitation: 'not only will the state be the "arbiter" of normal class struggle, and the primary opponent of class insurrection, but it may itself become directly implicated as the *object* of struggle between the classes'.[14] As we have seen, John Bosher, in his recent textbook on the Revolution, argues that 'A new Leviathan was born during the French Revolution', the modern French State. Certainly Bosher's approach differs significantly from that of a *marxisant* sociologist like George Comninel, but, to take just two areas spotlighted by Bosher, the massive expansion, indeed the very idea, of salaried civil servants, and the 'grand scale' of the Directory's dealings with war-suppliers and bankers, both underline the importance of the State as the dispenser of economic and political power.[15] Again, it was Karl Marx who wrote that 'The task of the first French Revolution was to destroy all separate local, territorial, urban and provincial powers in order to create the civil unity of the nation.'[16] Marx's interpretation of the Revolution has as much to do with the creation of the modern State as it has with the development of modern capitalism; the two were, of course, inter-dependent for him. William Doyle, again coming from the anti-marxist camp, has also stressed the fundamental importance, when considering the birth of the modern French State, of the abolition, following the decrees of August 1789, of 'the whole structure of provincial, local, and municipal government'.[17]

These few examples may be interpreted as a plea for a non-determinist, but not necessarily a non-ideological, approach to the study of the Revolution, premised upon the conviction that historical truth is relative rather than absolute. For if the marxist interpretation of history, supercharged with alarming nonsense like the 'dictatorship of the proletariat', has taken a severe drubbing over the past two decades, the revisionist onslaught, with its equally disturbing teleological, and ahistorical nonsense about Rousseau and Robespierre being the intellectual and philosophical forebears of Pol Pot, has failed to win a convincing majority. As Colin Jones has phrased it:'The Revisionist vulgate is a very negative one, more united in opposition to the old orthodoxy than in anything else.'[18] There is an intellectual sense of déjà-vu about sections of this particular Vulgate, a kind of 'L'année dernière à Ferney'. But, if any real meeting of minds is to be achieved, *marxisant* historians, or, at least, some of them, need to accept a more Thompsonian, yes, a more cultural 'history-as-process' approach, whilst revisionists need to remind themselves that social history is not, of necessity, the history of structurally determined, pre-ordained social classes.

My principal criticism of the contribution made by revisionists over the past two decades, and it is one shared by many British historians of the Revolution, marxist *and* non-marxist, concerns the way in which they have ignored or down-graded the importance of the social question during the 1790s. Deeply engaged in the ideological and intellectual struggle against marxism as some leading revisionists have been, one can readily understand why this should have happened: like the more politically charged marxist, they have allowed their ideological commitment or anti-marxist methodology to light their way to their libraries. Maybe this is not always a bad thing. The antagonisms, personal and political, between a Mathiez and an Aulard, or a Soboul and a Furet, have produced good historical fruit, even if they tasted rather bitter at times. It should always be remembered, however, that for the leaders of the Revolution, heirs of those applied social scientists, the *philosophes*, the social question remained at the top of the political agenda, at least until 1795, after which French society became increasingly bureaucratised and militarised. And, as Richard Cobb's brilliant forays into this field of history have shown, one does not have to wear a red, or even pink, tie to show a proper historical concern for the ordinary people who were the main sufferers of the revolutionary upheaval.

It *was* the involvement of peasants, artisans and shopkeepers which provided the main dynamic of the Revolution *during its early years*. Tim Blanning, as close to true revisionism as a good English, empiricist historian can possibly be, informs us that: 'If the bourgeois had had their way, the Revolution would have been closed down by 1791 at the latest. It was only insistent pressure from below which drove them on to destroy feudalism in its entirety.'[19] Throughout the 1790s, fear of 'popular despotism' fashioned the immediate political responses of politicians as well as the subsequent ideology of the liberal bourgeoisie. One should not dismiss this involvement, direct and indirect, of millions of French men and women as the actions of 'the chaotic people', or 'the arbitrary brutalities of the mob'.[20] There is a vast amount of work still to be completed on the social history of the Revolution. Let us give the last word to Ferenc Fehér, a revisionist historian who expressed his agreement with François Furet when the latter, in a recent lecture, expressed the desire for 'an act of reconciliation' – on the historiographical and political fronts – if modern democracy was to be successfully defended: 'I am in complete agreement with Furet's postulate, but I deem it feasible only on the basis of creating a legitimate space for the constant renegotiation of "the social question" on the basis of political freedom as an absolute precondition.'[21]

Notes

1 CAPITALISM, COLONIES AND THE CRISIS OF THE ANCIEN REGIME

1 P. Kennedy, *The Rise and Fall of the Great Powers*, London, Fontana, 1989, p. 147. See also J. Black, *The Rise of the European Powers 1679–1793*, London, Arnold, 1990, and ch. 1 of B. Stone, *The Genesis of the French Revolution: a Global-Historical Explanation*, Cambridge, Cambridge University Press, 1994.
2 T. Kaiser, 'Recent historiographical problems in relating the Enlightenment to the French Revolution', *French Historical Studies*, 15 (1988).
3 A. Soboul, *The French Revolution, 1787–1799: From the Storming of the Bastille to Napoleon*, London, Unwin Hyman, 1989, p. 28.
4 A. Young, *Travels in France during the Years 1787,1788 and 1789*, ed. J. Kaplow, Gloucester, Mass., P. Smith, 1976, p. 57.
5 J. Lough (ed.), *France on the Eve of the Revolution: British Travellers' Observations, 1763–1788*, London, Croom Helm, 1987, p. 89.
6 D. Roche (ed.), *The People of Paris: An Essay on Popular Culture in the Eighteenth Century*, Leamington Spa, Berg Press, 1987, pp. 185–6.
7 L-S. Mercier, *Le Tableau de Paris*, Geneva, Slatkine Reprints, 1979, vol. ii, p. 214.
8 S. Pollard, *Peaceful Conquest and the Industrialization of Europe, 1760–1970*, Oxford, Oxford University Press, 1981.
9 E. Labrousse, *La Crise de l'économie française*, Paris, Presses Universitaires de France, 1944, pp. 472–3.
10 See F. Crouzet, *De la supériorité de l'Angleterre sur la France: l'économique et l'imaginaire, XVIIe–XXe siècles*, Paris, Perrin, 1985, p. 32.
11 T. Blanning, *The French Revolution: Aristocrats versus Bourgeois?* London, Macmillan, 1989, p. 11.
12 G. Lewis, *The Advent of Modern Capitalism in France 1770–1840: The Contribution of Pierre-François Tubeuf*, Oxford, Oxford University Press, 1993.
13 T. Blanning, *The French Revolution*, p. 17.
14 *A Social History of French Catholicism, 1789–1914*, London, Routledge, 1989, ch.1.
15 W. Doyle, *The Oxford History of the French Revolution*, Oxford, Oxford University Press, 1989, pp. 22–3.
16 M. Forsyth, *Reason and Revolution: The Political Thought of the abbé Sieyès*, Leicester, Leicester University Press, 1987, pp. 82–3.
17 *The French Nobility in the Eighteenth Century: from Feudalism to*

Enlightenment, trans. William Doyle, Cambridge, Cambridge University Press, 1985, p. 42.

18 *Past and Present*, 60 (1973).

19 M. Sonenscher, *Work and Wages: Natural Law, Politics and the Eighteenth-Century French Trades*, Cambridge, Cambridge University Press, 1989, p. 67.

20 *The Peasantry in the French Revolution*, Cambridge, Cambridge University Press, 1988, p. 14.

21 L-S. Mercier, *Tableau de Paris*, vol. i, p. 55.

2 THE BIRTH OF THE REPUBLIC, 1787–92

1 J. Bosher, *The French Revolution*, London, Weidenfeld & Nicolson, 1989, p. 46.

2 K. Baker, *Interpreting the French Revolution*, Cambridge, Cambridge University Press, 1990, p. 140. See also W. Doyle, 'The Parlements', in K. Baker (ed.), *The French Revolution and the Creation of Modern Political Culture*, Oxford, Pergamon, 1987, vol. 1, *The Political Culture of the Old Régime*, pp. 157–67.

3 T. Blanning, *The Origins of the French revolutionary Wars*, London, Longman, 1986, p. 42.

4 W. Doyle, *The Oxford History of the French Revolution*, Oxford, Oxford University Press, 1989, p. 66.

5 G. Claeys, *Thomas Paine, Social and Political Thought*, London, Unwin Hyman, 1989, p. 26.

6 J. Popkin, *Revolutionary News: The Press in France*, London, Duke University Press, 1990, pp. 25–6. See also H. Gough, *The Newspaper Press in the French Revolution*, London, Routledge, 1988.

7 A. Soboul, *The French Revolution 1787–1799: From the Storming of the Bastille to Napoleon*, London, Unwin Hyman, 1989.

8 F. Furet, 'La Monarchie et le règlement électoral de 1789', in *The Political Culture of the Old Regime*, ed. K. Baker, pp. 375–86.

9 M. Forsyth, *Reason and Revolution: the Political Thought of the abbé Sieyès*, Leicester, Leicester University Press, 1987, p. 82.

10 P. R. Hanson, *Provincial Politics in the French Revolution: Caen and Limoges, 1789–1794*, Baton Rouge, Louisiana State University Press, 1989, pp. 31–2.

11 R. Laurent and G. Gavignaud, *La Révolution française dans le Languedoc méditerranéen*, Toulouse, Privat, 1987, p. 39.

12 P. Jones, *The Peasantry in the French Revolution*, Cambridge, Cambridge University Press, 1988, p. 71.

13 W. Doyle, *Oxford History*, p. 117.

14 R. Griffiths, *Le Centre perdu: Malouet et les monarchiens dans la Révolution française*, Grenoble, Presses Universitaires, 1988, p. 95.

15 See C. L. James, *The Black Jacobins: Toussaint L'Ouverture and the San Domingo Revolution*, London, Allison & Busby, 1982.

16 S. Scott, *The Response of the Royal Army to the French Revolution: The Role and Development of the Line Army, 1787–1793*, Oxford, Oxford University Press, 1978, p. 109.

3 WAR, REVOLUTION AND THE RISE OF THE NATION-STATE, 1792–9

1 T. Blanning, *The Origins of the Revolutionary Wars*, London, Longman, 1986, p. 69.
2 F. Furet, 'Revolutionary government', in F. Furet and M. Ozouf (eds), *A Critical Dictionary of the French Revolution*, Cambridge, Mass., Harvard University Press, 1989, p. 550.
3 C. J. Mitchell, *The French Legislative Assembly of 1791*, Leiden, E. J. Brill, 1988, p. 229.
4 A. Goodwin, *The Friends of Liberty: The English Democratic Movement in the Age of the French Revolution*, London, Hutchinson, 1979, p. 247.
5 W. D. Edmonds, *Jacobinism and the Revolt of Lyon, 1789–1793*, Oxford, Oxford University Press, 1990, p. 133.
6 G. Rudé (ed.), *Robespierre*, Englewood Cliffs, NJ, Prentice-Hall, 1967, p. 27.
7 J. Lynn, *The Bayonets of the Republic: Motivation and Tactics in the Army of Revolutionary France, 1791–1794*, Chicago, University of Illinois Press, 1984, pp. 53–7.
8 P. R. Hanson, *Provincial Politics in the French Revolution*, Baton Rouge, Louisiana State University Press, 1989, p. 244.
9 C. J. Mitchell, *The French Legislative Assembly*, pp. 206–7.
10 A. Sa'adah, *The Shaping of Liberal Politics in Revolutionary France: A Comparative Perspective*, Princeton, Princeton University Press, 1990, p. 187.
11 M. Kennedy, *The Jacobin Club in The French Revolution: The Middle Years*, Princeton, Princeton University Press, 1988, pp. 366–7.
12 R. C. Cobb, *The People's Armies*, trans. M. Elliott, New Haven, Yale University Press, 1987, p. 458.
13 W. Markov and A. Soboul (eds), *Die Sansculotten von Paris*, Berlin, Akademie Verlag, 1957, p. 208.
14 C. Lucas, *The Structure of the Terror: The Example of Javogues in the Loire*, Oxford, Oxford University Press, 1973, pp. 284–86.
15 D. P. Jordan, *The Revolutionary Career of Maximilian Robespierre*, New York, Free Press, 1985, p. 192.
16 F. Furet, 'Terror', in Furet and Ozouf (eds), *A Critical Dictionary*, pp. 148–50.
17 A. Soboul, *The French Revolution 1787–1799*, London, Unwin Hyman, 1989, pp. 414–15.
18 *The French Revolution*, London, Weidenfeld & Nicolson, 1989, ch. xi, 'A new Leviathan'.
19 *The Oxford History of the French Revolution*, Oxford, Oxford University Press, 1989, p. 281.
20 *Origins of the Revolutionary Wars*, p. 197.
21 R. B. Rose, *Gracchus Babeuf: The First Revolutionary Communist*, London, E. Arnold, 1978, pp. 329–45.
22 T. Skocpol and M. Kestnbaum, 'Mars unshackled: the French Revolution in world-historical perspective', in F. Fehér (ed.), *The French Revolution and the Birth of Modernity*, Berkeley, University of California Press, 1990, p. 25.

23 See D. Sutherland, *The Chouans; The Social Origins of the Popular Counter-Revolution in Upper Brittany, 1770–1796*, Oxford, Oxford University Press, 1982, and G. Lewis, 'Political brigandage and popular disaffection in the south-east of France, 1795–1804', in G. Lewis and C. Lucas (eds), *Beyond the Terror: Essays in French Regional and Social History, 1794–1815*, Cambridge, Cambridge University Press, 1983.

24 Isser Woloch, 'The State and the villages in revolutionary France', in *Reshaping France: Town, Country and Region during the French Revolution*, A. Forrest and P. Jones (eds), Manchester, Manchester University Press, 1991, p. 227.

25 ' "Aux urnes, citoyens!" Urban and rural electoral behaviour during the French Revolution', in *Reshaping France*, p. 164.

26 M. Forsyth, *Reason and Revolution*, Leicester, Leicester University Press, 1987, p. 193.

4 THE POLITICAL ECONOMY OF THE REVOLUTION

1 See, for example, F. Aftalion, *The French Revolution: An Economic Interpretation*, Cambridge, Cambridge University Press, 1990.

2 *La Révolution française et l'économie: décollage ou catastrophe*, Paris, Editions Nathan, 1989, p. 137.

3 *Citizens: A Chronicle of the French Revolution*, London, Viking Press, 1989, pp. 190–1.

4 *The Oxford History of the French Revolution*, Oxford, Oxford University Press, 1989, pp. 12–13.

5 P. Jones, *The Peasantry in the French Revolution*, Cambridge, Cambridge University Press, 1988, p. 33.

6 F. Hincker, *La Révolution française*, p. 43.

7 R. Sédillot, *Le coût de la Révolution française*, Paris, Perrin, 1987, pp. 178–81.

8 F. Hincker, *La Révolution française*, pp. 44–6.

9 See G. Lewis, *The Advent of Modern Capitalism in France, 1770–1840*, Oxford, Oxford University Press, 1993, ch. 2.

10 P. Jones, *The Peasantry*, pp. 42–9.

11 *The Coming of the French Revolution*, trans. R. R. Palmer, Princeton, Princeton University Press, 1969, p. 210.

12 Aftalion, *The French Revolution*, p. 103.

13 ibid., p. 1.

14 *La Révolution française*, pp. 136–7.

15 J. Bosher, *French Finances, 1770–1795: From Business to Bureaucracy*, Cambridge, Cambridge University Press, 1970.

16 *Robespierre: politique et mystique*, Paris, Editions du Seuil, 1987, pp. 333–9.

17 M. Brugière, *Gestionnaires et profiteurs de la Révolution*, Paris, O. Orban, 1986. See, in particular, pp. 116–32.

18 P. Jones, *The Peasantry*, p. 121.

19 N. Hampson, *Saint-Just*, Oxford, Oxford University Press, pp. 90–1.

20 R. C. Cobb, *The People's Armies*, trans. M. Elliott, New Haven, Yale University Press, 1987, pp. 254–9.

21 *Saint-Just*, p. 178.
22 *The French Revolution*, p. 179.
23 F. Hincker, *La Révolution française*, p. 152.
24 H. Bonin, 'La Révolution française, a-t-elle brisée l'esprit d'entreprise?', *Information historique*, 47 (1985), p. 198.
25 A. Brosselin, A Corvol and F. Vion-Delphin, 'Les Doléances contre l'industrie', in D. Woronoff (ed.), *Forges et forêts: recherches sur la consommation proto-industrielle de bois*, Paris, Editions de l'Ecole des Hautes Etudes, 1990, p. 22.
26 G. Lewis, *The Advent of Modern Capitalism in France*, pp. 339.
27 See F. Crouzet, 'Guerres, blocus et changement économique, 1792–1815', in *De la supériorité de l'Angleterre sur la France: l'économique et l'imaginaire, XVIIe–XXe siècles*, Paris, Perrin, 1985.
28 See G. Lemarchand, 'La Féodalité et la Révolution: seigneurie et communauté paysanne', *Annales historiques de la Révolution française*, 52 (1980).

5 SOCIAL INTERPRETATIONS OF THE REVOLUTION

1 *The Social Interpretation of the French Revolution*, Cambridge, Cambridge University Press, 1964.
2 C. Jones, *The Longman Companion to the French Revolution*, London, Longman, 1988, pp. 287–8.
3 *Peasantry and Society in France Since 1789*, Cambridge, Cambridge University Press, 1991, p. 15.
4 *The Oxford History of the French Revolution*, Oxford, Oxford University Press, 1989, p. 117.
5 See my introduction to Soboul's *The French Revolution, 1787–1799*, London, Unwin Hyman, 1989, pp. xi–xxviii.
6 *La Révolution française et l'économie*, Paris, Editions Nathan, 1989, p. 103.
7 P. Jones, *The Peasantry in the French Revolution*, Cambridge, Cambridge University Press, 1988, p. 157.
8 T. Le Goff and D. Sutherland, 'The Revolution and the rural economy', in A. Forrest and P. Jones (eds), *Reshaping France: Town, Country and Region during the French Revolution*, Manchester, Manchester University Press, 1991, p. 76.
9 G. Bourgin, *Le partage des biens communaux. Documents sur la préparation de la loi du juin 1793*, Paris, 1908, pp. 470–1.
10 D. Lovell, 'The French Revolution and the origins of socialism: the case of early French socialism', *French History*, 6 (1992).
11 P. Jones, 'The Agrarian Law and schemes for land redistribution during the French Revolution', *Past and Present*, 133 (1991), p. 132.
12 *The Napoleonic Empire*, London, Macmillan, 1991, p. 14.
13 D. Sutherland, *The Chouans: The Social Origins of the Popular Counter-Revolution in Upper Brittany, 1770–1796*, Oxford, Oxford University Press, 1982, p. 19.
14 G. Lewis, 'Les Egorgeurs du département du Gard: analyse du mouvement Catholique royaliste sous le Directoire et le Consulat', in *Religion,*

Révolution, Contre-révolution dans le Midi, 1789–1799, Nîmes, J. Chambon, 1991.
15 'The Revolution and the rural economy', p. 75.
16 Cited in D. Sutherland, *The Chouans*, p. 10.
17 'Compagnonnage, confraternities, and associations of journeymen in eighteenth-century Paris', *European History Quarterly*, 16 (1986), p. 40.
18 D. Roche (ed.), *Journal of My Life: Jacques-Louis Ménétra*, New York, Columbia University Press, 1986.
19 Michael Sonescher, 'Artisans, *sans-culottes* and the French Revolution', in A. Forrest and P. Jones (eds), *Reshaping France*, p. 109.
20 *Artisans and Sansculottes: Popular Movements in France and Britain during the French Revolution*, London, 1989, p. xlii.
21 *The French Revolution*, pp. 48–9.
22 *The French Nobility in the Eighteenth-Century*, trans. W. Doyle, Cambridge, Cambridge University Press, 1985, p. 87.
23 'Popular sovereignty and executive power in the Federalist Revolt of 1793', *French History*, 5 (1991), p. 75.
24 *Provincial Politics in the French Revolution*, Baton Rouge, Louisiana State University Press, 1989, p. 246.
25 *Jacobinism and the Revolt of Lyon, 1789–1793*, Oxford, Oxford University Press, 1990, p. 281.
26 'Popular sovereignty and executive power', p. 96.
27 H. Brown, 'A discredited regime: the Directory and army contracting', *French History*, 4 (1990), p. 76.
28 'Revolution and the urban economy: maritime cities and continental cities', in A. Forrest and P. Jones (eds), *Reshaping France*, p. 47.
29 *The Politics of Privilege*, Cambridge, Cambridge University Press, 1991, p. 183.
30 See L. Bergeron, *Banquiers, négociants et manufacturiers parisiens du Directoire à l'Empire*, Paris, 1978.
31 *Gestionnaires et profiteurs de la Révolution*, Paris, O. Orban, 1986, pp. 227–93.
32 Cited by L. Chevalier, *Labouring Classes and Dangerous Classes in Paris during the First Half of the Nineteenth Century*, London, Routledge & Kegan Paul, 1973, p. 221.
33 A. Forrest, *The Poor in the French Revolution*, Oxford, Oxford University Press, 1981, p. 26.
34 *Death in Paris, 1795–1801*, Oxford, Oxford University Press, 1978. See, in particular, ch. 4.
35 *The Poor in the French Revolution*, p. 170.
36 *Artisans and Sansculottes*, p. xxxii.
37 See G. Levy, H. Applewhite, M. Johnson (eds), *Women in Revolutionary Paris, 1789–1795*, Illinois, University of Chicago Press, 1979; and O. Hufton, *Women and the Limits of Citizenship in the French Revolution*, Toronto, Toronto University Press, 1992.
38 G. Bossenga, *The Politics of Privilege*, p. 154.
39 C. Thomas, 'Heroism in the feminine' in S. Petrey (ed.), *The French Revolution, 1789–1989: Two Hundred Years of Rethinking*, Texas, Texas Tech. University Press, 1989.
40 See H. Mills, ' "Recasting the Pantheon"'? Women and the French

Revolution', in C. Jones (ed.), *The French Revolution in Perspective*, Nottingham, Nottingham University Press, 1989.

6 REVOLUTIONARY CULTURE: THE CREATION OF *'L'HOMME NOUVEAU'*

1 E. Kennedy, *A Cultural History of the French Revolution*, New Haven, Yale University Press, 1989, p. 1.
2 'Introduction: meaning in action, action in meaning', in S. Petrey (ed.), *The French Revolution, 1789–1989*, Texas, Texas Tech. University Press, 1989, p. 4.
3 'Babeuf's candour: the rhetorical invention of a prophet', in J. Renwick (ed.), *Language and Rhetoric of the Revolution*, Edinburgh, Edinburgh University Press, 1990, p. 85.
4 'Discourses of patriarchalism and anti-patriarchalism in the French Revolution', in J. Renwick (ed.), *Language and Rhetoric*, p. 26.
5 *Politics, Culture and Class in the French Revolution*, London, Methuen, 1986, p. 177.
6 ' "Aristocrate", "Aristocratie": language and politics in the French Revolution', in S. Petrey (ed.), *The French Revolution*, p. 63.
7 J. McManners, *Death and the Enlightenment; Changing Attitudes to Death among Christians and Unbelievers in Eighteenth-Century France*, Oxford, Oxford University Press, 1981, p. 462.
8 R. Gibson, *A Social History of French Catholicism, 1789–1914*, London, Routledge, 1989, p. 2.
9 S. Eliot and B. Stern, *The Age of the Enlightenment; An Anthology of Eighteenth-Century Texts*, East Grinstead, Open University, 1979, vol. 2, p. 131.
10 ibid., p. 165.
11 *A Social History of French Catholicism*, p. 40.
12 T. Tackett, *Religion, Revolution and Regional Culture in Eighteenth Century France: The Ecclesiastical Oath of 1791*, Princeton, Princeton University Press, 1986, pp. 288–300.
13 R. Gibson, *A Social History of French Catholicism*, p. 53.
14 G. Rudé (ed.), *Robespierre*, New Jersey, Prentice-Hall, 1967, p. 71.
15 'The reconstruction of a church, 1798–1801', in G. Lewis and C. Lucas (eds), *Beyond the Terror*, Cambridge, Cambridge University Press, 1983.
16 R. Gibson, *A Social History of French Catholicism*, p. 55.
17 'Regeneration', in F. Furet and M. Ozouf (eds), *A Critical Dictionary of the French Revolution*, Cambridge, Mass., Harvard University Press, 1978, p. 785.
18 *The Oxford History of the French Revolution*, Oxford, Oxford University Press, 1989, p. 399.
19 C. Hesse, *Publishing and Cultural Politics in Revolutionary Paris, 1789–1810*, Berkeley, University of California Press, 1991, p. 80.
20 *Space and Revolution: Projects for Monuments, Squares and Public Buildings in France, 1789–1799*, Montreal, McGill/Queens University Press, 1991, p. 27.
21 ibid., p. 266.

22 P. Bordes, *David*, Paris, F. Hazan, 1988, p. 60.
23 J. Leith, *Space and Revolution*, pp. 233–4.
24 M. Ozouf, *La Fête Révolutionnaire, 1789–1799*, Paris, Gallimard, 1976.
25 J. Leith, *Space and Revolution*, pp. 130–4.
26 L. Hunt, *Politics, Culture and Class in the French Revolution*, London, Methuen, 1986, p. 111.
27 M. Carlson, *The Theatre of the French Revolution*, New York, Cornell University Press, 1966, pp. 176–7.
28 *Politics, Culture and Class*, p. 116.
29 M. Gauchet, 'Constant', in F. Furet and M. Ozouf (eds), *A Critical Dictionary of the French Revolution*, p. 926.
30 'L'Expérience Thermidorienne', in C. Lucas (ed.), *The Political Culture of the French Revolution*, Oxford, Pergamon Press, 1988, p. 365.

CONCLUSION

1 *The Prelude* ed. E. de Seligman, Oxford, Oxford University Press, 1970, Book IX, ll, 178–83.
2 G. Rudé (ed.), *Robespierre*, New Jersey, Prentice-Hall, 1967, p. 69.
3 'State, nation, and class in the French Revolution', in F. Fehér (ed.), *The French Revolution and the Birth of Modernity*, Berkeley, University of California Press, 1990, p. 122.
4 'Introduction', in K. Baker (ed.), *The Political Culture of the Old Regime*, Oxford, Pergamon Press, 1987, p. xxiii.
5 *The French Nobility in the Eighteenth Century*, trans. W. Doyle, Cambridge, Cambridge University Press, 1985, p. 106.
6 *Comprendre la Révolution: problèmes politiques de la Révolution française*, Paris, Maspero, 1976.
7 *The French Revolution, 1787–1799*, London, Unwin Hyman, 1989, p. 3.
8 E. Thompson, *The Poverty of Theory and Other Essays*, London, Merlin Press, 1978. R. Robin, *La Société française en 1789: Semur-en-Auxois*, Paris, 1970.
9 *The French Revolution: Aristocrats versus Bourgeois?* London, Macmillan, 1989, p. 16.
10 See, for example, 'Artisans versus Fabricants: urban protoindustrialisation and the evolution of work culture in Lodève and Bédarieux, 1740–1830', European University Institute (Florence) Working Paper, no. 85/137, n.d.
11 G. Comninel, *Rethinking the French Revolution: Marxism and the Revisionist Challenge*, London, Verso Books, 1987.
12 For the remainder of this section of the argument see ibid., pp. 196–200.
13 *Past and Present* 60 (1973).
14 ibid., p. 172.
15 *The French Revolution*, London, Weidenfeld & Nicolson, 1989, see chapter eleven.
16 G. Comninel, *Rethinking the French Revolution*, p. 203.
17 *The Oxford History of the French Revolution*, Oxford, Oxford University Press, 1989, p. 117.
18 'Revisionism, post-revisionism, and new perspectives on the French

Revolution', in C. Jones (ed.), *The French Revolution in Perspective*, Nottingham, University of Nottingham Press, 1989, p. iii.
19 *The French Revolution*, p. 3.
20 S. Schama, *Citizens: a Chronicle of the French Revolution*, London, Viking Press, 1989, pp. 748 and 648.
21 *The Birth of Modernity*, p. 7.

Select bibliography

Aftalion, F. (1990) *The French Revolution: An Economic Interpretation*, Cambridge, Cambridge University Press. A monetarist account of the economic history of the Revolution.

Baker, K. (1990) *Interpreting the French Revolution*, Cambridge, Cambridge University Press. A collection of articles which prioritise the political and the cultural, by one of the leading revisionist, intellectual historians.

—— (ed.) (1987) *The French Revolution and the Creation of Modern Political Culture*, vol. 1, *The Political Culture of the Old Regime*, Oxford, Pergamon Press. The 'Chicago School' of revisionist historians offer their interpretations of the Revolution.

Blanning, T. (1989) *The French Revolution: Aristocrats versus Bourgeois?*, London, Macmillan. Short, sparky, and neo-revisionist.

Bosher, J. (1989) *The French Revolution*, London, Weidenfeld & Nicolson. An original textbook which shadows the revisionist line: good chapters on the State and the economy.

Bossenga, G. (1991) *The Politics of Privilege: Old Regime and Revolution in Lille*, Cambridge, Cambridge University Press. Refreshingly new approach, focusing particularly on fiscal matters, to the relationship between Paris and a major, textile town.

Brugière, M. (1986) *Gestionnaires et profiteurs de la Révolution*, Paris, O. Orban. Most welcome addition to our knowledge of the financial elites during the Revolution. Very useful 'pen-portraits'.

Chaussinand-Nogaret, G. (1985) *The French Nobility in the Eighteenth Century: From Feudalism to Enlightenment*, trans. W. Doyle, Cambridge, Cambridge University Press. Original, but ultimately unconvincing account of the 'revolutionary' role of the French nobility in the creation of an eighteenth-century 'elite', central to the revisionist, anti-marxist case.

Cobb, R. (1978) *Death in Paris, 1795–1801*, Oxford, Oxford University Press. Death visited by one of the great social historians of the Revolution.

—— (1987) *The People's Armies*, trans. M. Elliott, New Haven, Yale University Press. Classic work on the 'Popular Movement-in-Arms'.

Cobban, A. (1964) *The Social Interpretation of the French Revolution*, Cambridge, Cambridge University Press. The 'father of revisionism' asks the right questions about the marxist interpretation of the Revolution and offers wrong answers.

Comninel, G. (1987) *Rethinking The French Revolution: Marxism and the*

Revisionist Challenge, London, Verso Books. An uneasy, but challenging, attempt to marry historical materialism to revisionism.

Crouzet, F. (1985) *De la supériorité de l'Angleterre sur la France: l'économique et l'imaginaire, XVIIe–XXe siècles*, Paris, Perrin. Collection of articles by one of the leading French economic historians.

Doyle, W. (1989) *The Oxford History of the French Revolution*, Oxford, Oxford University Press. Judicious, comprehensive, and balanced, a fine example of the English, liberal, empiricist tradition, revisionist in tone rather than in content.

Edmonds, W. (1990) *Jacobinism and the Revolt of Lyon, 1789–1793*, Oxford, Oxford University Press. Distinguished by its research base and its dialectical account of the Paris–Lyon tragedy.

Fehér, F. (ed.) (1990) *The French Revolution and the Birth of Modernity*, Berkeley, University of California Press. The most interesting of the many collections of articles conceived during the Bicentennial commemoration of the Revolution, with contributions from historians as ideologically divided as Eric Hobsbawm and François Furet.

Forrest, A. (1981) *The Poor in the French Revolution*, Oxford, Oxford University Press. General survey of the major social problem confronting the Revolution.

—— and Jones, P. (eds) (1991) *Reshaping France: Town, Country and Region During the French Revolution*, Manchester, Manchester University Press. A wide range of historians discussing a wide range of topics.

Furet, F. and Ozouf, M. (eds) (1989) *A Critical Dictionary of the French Revolution*, Cambridge, Mass., Harvard University Press. 'Write-bites' of the Revolution from a revisionist angle – 'actors', 'events', 'institutions', etc. Few peasants to be seen in its 1,000 pages.

Gibson, R. (1989) *A Social History of French Catholicism, 1789–1914*, London, Routledge. The best general account of the impact of Catholicism upon nineteenth-century French society.

Gough, H. (1988) *The Newspaper Press in the French Revolution*, London, Routledge. Very good survey of recent work on the revolutionary Press, Parisian *and* provincial.

Hanson, P. (1989) *Provincial Politics in the French Revolution: Caen and Limoges, 1789–1794*, Baton Rouge, Louisiana State University Press. Thoughtful, comparative study of two provincial towns.

Hesse, C. (1991) *Publishing and Cultural Politics in Revolutionary Paris 1789–1810*, Berkeley, University of California Press. Proves that one can write cultural history without ignoring political *and* economic issues.

Hincker, F. (1989) *La Révolution française et l'économie: décollage ou catastrophe?*, Paris, Editions Nathan. Useful quantitative and qualitative account; a corrective to Aftalion's thesis.

Hunt, L. (1986) *Politics, Culture and Class in the French Revolution*, London, Methuen. The best kind of revisionist history – provocative, original, intellectually stimulating.

Jones, C. (1988) *The Longman Companion to the French Revolution*, London, Longman. Indispensable filofax of the Revolution.

Jones, P. (1988) *The Peasantry in the French Revolution*, Cambridge, Cambridge University Press. Excellent survey of the impact of the Revolution upon the peasantry.

Kennedy, E. (1989) *A Cultural History of the French Revolution*, New Haven, Yale University Press. A very readable textbook which incorporates recent research on the subject.

Leith, J. (1991) *Space and Revolution: Projects for Monuments, Squares and Public Buildings in France, 1789–1799*, Montreal, McGill/Queen's University Press. The architecture of the revolutionary imagination, complete with 361 illustrations.

Lewis, G. (1993) *The Advent of Modern Capitalism in France, 1770–1840: The Contribution of Pierre-François Tubeuf*, Oxford, Oxford University Press. The epic struggle of a dynamic, but forgotten, entrepreneur to introduce modern mining to the 'post-feudal' society of the Basses-Cévennes region.

—— and Lucas, C. (eds) (1983) *Beyond the Terror: Essays in French Regional and Social History, 1794–1815*, Cambridge, Cambridge University Press. Essays which underline the major contribution of British historians to the provincial history of France during the Directory and Consulate.

Lucas, C. (1973) *The Structure of the Terror: The Example of Javogues in the Loire*, Oxford, Oxford University Press. Reveals, in some detail, the interdependent cogs of the machinery of repression in the provinces,

—— (ed.) (1988) *The French Revolution and the Creation of Modern Political Culture*, vol. 2, *The Political Culture of the French Revolution*, Oxford, Pergamon Press. Another twenty-three reasons why we should believe in the new revisionism.

Lynn, J. (1984) *The Bayonets of the Republic: Motivation and Tactics in the Army of Revolutionary France, 1791–1794*, Chicago, University of Illinois Press. Military history at its best.

Lyons, M. (1975) *France under the Directory*, Cambridge, Cambridge University Press. Still one of the best general surveys of the period.

Petrey, S. (ed.) (1989) *The French Revolution, 1789–1989: Two Hundred Years of Rethinking*, Texas, Texas Tech. University Press. Articles which raise the symbolic and semiotic to the top of the agenda of revolutionary studies.

Roberts, J. (1990) *The Counter-revolution in France, 1787–1830*, London, Macmillan. Thoughtful and novel approach to the topic.

Roche, D. (ed.) (1987) *The People of Paris: An Essay on Popular Culture in the Eighteenth Century*, Leamington Spa, Berg Press. Original essay on the impact of a nascent 'consumer culture' on the popular masses.

Rose, R. (1978) *Gracchus Babeuf: The First Revolutionary Communist*, London, E. Arnold. The best account in English of Babeuf's life and ideas.

Schama, S. (1989) *Citizens: A Chronicle of the French Revolution*, London, Viking Press. A blockbuster, with some brilliant *aperçus*, from an historian who treats 'the people' with Voltairian contempt.

Scott, S. (1978) *The Response of the Royal Army to the French Revolution: The Role and Development of the Line Army, 1787–1793*, Oxford, Oxford University Press. One of the best social histories of the *ancien régime* and revolutionary armies.

Scott, W. (1973) *Terror and Repression in Revolutionary Marseilles*, London. One of the best accounts of the Terror in the provinces.

Soboul, A. (1989) *The French Revolution, 1787–1799: From the Storming of the Bastille to Napoleon*, London, Unwin Hyman. *The* classic *marxisant* textbook on the Revolution; far less determinist than some critics suggest.

Sonenscher, M. (1989) *Work and Wages: Natural Law, Politics and the Eighteenth-Century French Trades*, Cambridge, Cambridge University Press. Well-researched, intellectually stimulating, neo-revisionist.

Sutherland, D. (1982) *The Chouans: the Social Origins of the Popular Counter-Revolution in Upper Brittany, 1770–1796*, Oxford, Oxford University Press. A good example of the socio-economic approach to the counter-revolution.

Tackett, T. (1986) *Religion, Revolution and Regional Culture in Eighteenth Century France: The Ecclesiastical Oath of 1791*, Princeton, Princeton University Press. Subtle, scholarly analysis of the problems surrounding the Civil Constitution of the Clergy and its implementation.

Index